In the Service of His Country

The Biography of Dasang Damdul Tsarong, Commander General of Tibet

In the Service of His Country

The Biography of Dasang Damdul Tsarong, Commander General of Tibet

by
Dundul Namgyal Tsarong

edited by
Ani Trinlay Chodron

Snow Lion Publications
Ithaca, New York USA

Snow Lion Publications
605 West State Street
P. O. Box 6483
Ithaca, NY 14851
(607) 273-8519
www.snowlionpub.com

Library of Congress Cataloging-in-Publication Data

Tsarong, Dundul Namgyal, 1920-
    In the service of his country : the biography of Dasang Damdul Tsarong,
commander general of Tibet / by Dundul Namgyal Tsarong.
          p.   cm.
      ISBN 1-55939-151-0
    1. Tsarong, Dasang Damdul, 1888-1959. 2. Generals—China—Tibet—
Biography. 3. Tibet (China)—History. I. Title.
DS786 .T6748 2000
951'.505'092—dc21

                                                                00-009142

Contents

Foreword

Dasang Damdul Tsarong dedicated his life to the service of Tibet. His quick intelligence and ability came early to the notice of
my predecessor, the Thirteenth Dalai Lama. In due course he
became a Cabinet Minister and Commander-in-Chief of the Tibetan army. A shrewd and acute man, he learned a great deal
when he accompanied the Thirteenth Dalai Lama to the Tibetans of Mongolia, to China and later to India, becoming one of
the few Tibetans of the time to have an idea of the wider world.
Despite opposition from more conservative factions, Tsarong had
a great desire to employ his innovative bent for the good of Tibet at large.

   Although he is most often remembered as a hero for his part
in defeating Chinese troops pursuing the Thirteenth Dalai Lama
as he escaped to India in 1910, his contribution to Tibetan life
was far-reaching in many other ways. In his courage, loyalty,
candor and single-mindedness, as well as his devotion to his
adopted family, Dasang Damdul Tsarong embodied many of the
best qualities of old Tibet. In an era beset by intrigues he accepted the vicissitudes of power with good grace, continuing to
proffer sound advice whenever it was sought.

   In this book, Dasang Damdul Tsarong's son gives an account
of his father's life. Naturally, it also sheds light on the years of
Tibet's declared independence and the period that culminated
in its final occupation by the Communist Chinese. It is sad to
note that Tsarong was one of the many who perished under

Chinese imprisonment. But it is fitting that this Tibetan patriot did not long survive the tragedy of occupation to see the destruction of all that he held dear.

—His Holiness the Dalai Lama

1 In the Household of the Thirteenth Dalai Lama

A seventeen-year-old boy turned his horse up the mountain, sensing an attack by a group of Golok men armed with spears. These men from Amdo province annually traveled from their homeland to visit the holy city of Lhasa and make offerings to the sacred image of Jowo Rinpoche, an image of the Lord Buddha in the Central Temple, or *Tsuglak Khang*. Having shot a few rounds with his Mauser pistol in the air to discourage the assumed attackers, he resumed his journey towards Lhasa. He was on leave from the Dalai Lama's court and was now returning to resume his duties at the Norbu Lingka Palace. This was my father, Dasang Damdul Tsarong, who was to serve Tibet faithfully throughout his life. He was born in a house named Khakhor Shi in Phenpo Province. It stood in a small village situated to the north of Lhasa. There were many prominent family homes there—Jorden Khangsar, Magshok Gangpa, Changra Sharpa, Dhargye Khangsar, and Tharpa Ling. Others belonged to the common laborers and field workers.

Phenpo, a beautiful and fertile valley situated to the northeast of Lhasa, the capital city of Tibet, was the birthplace of my father. It is a two-day horseback journey from the city. One of the highest passes in Central Tibet, Phenpo Ghola, must be crossed during this trip and almost a whole day is spent ascending and descending the Ghola before one reaches Phenpo. In winter, about two feet of snow falls on the pass, but it is soon melted away by the sun. The temperature in the town averages between seventy and seventy-five degrees Fahrenheit in summer, and in winter, between twenty-five and forty degrees. Its altitude is approximately 12,500 feet above sea level. This fertile valley is surrounded by hills covered with beautiful wild alpine flowers in late spring, and with many wild animals, such as mountain sheep, goats, leopards, and gazelles. Moreover, it is a valley where century-old monasteries, such as Shawa Bhonpa, Langthang, and Gaden Chokhor, to mention a few, have been consecrated. Pilgrims come from several nearby villages and towns to pay homage to these monasteries.

The people of Phenpo are intelligent, brave, self-sufficient, and content. They are also good sportsmen, especially skilled in riding and archery. There is an old saying which runs, "There is no need for Aku Tonpa where resources of intelligence are adequate."

This remark is said to have been made by a man named Aku Tonpa when he visited Phenpo from his birthplace, Dechen. Aku Tonpa is famous in Tibet for roaming about in provinces adjacent to Dechen, showing his high intelligence and sense of humor by amusing his hosts with jokes and stories.

Phenpo people are also most skillful in crafts. They weave their own woolen cloth for their dresses and sew their own woolen boots. At least one member of a family is highly skilled in weaving or sewing.

The dialect of the Phenpo region is the same as that of Central Tibet, with just a few words having a different pronunciation. The written language is the same throughout the country, and it is read and understood from east to west and north to south. The predominant religion is Buddhism and the people are very pious. Offerings are made to every temple and monastery, and even the poorest family will have an altar and an offering of a butter lamp in its home. The vocation of these people is usually agricultural in nature. The main products of the valley are barley, wheat, peas, potatoes, and mustard.

Phenpo is famous for its production of mustard oil, which is the main cooking medium used by Tibetans. Mustard oil is packed and sewn in sheep skins and transported to Lhasa and the nearby towns on mules, donkeys, and yaks. Besides farming the land, animal husbandry is widespread. Yaks, cows, sheep, goats, and *dzomo*, which are a crossbreed of yaks and cows, are kept by the farmers. *Yubel*, the soft sheep-wool of Phenpo, is known to be the best wool in Tibet.

My father was born in Khakhor Shi, a peasant home, in the year 1888. His mother's name was Yudon, and his father, Thondup Gyalpo, was also known as Aku Dazo, meaning "Uncle Arrow Maker." Besides engaging in agriculture, my grandfather had a hobby and business making bows and arrows. He was a skilled arrow maker and a skilled archer.

Phenpo people were well known for archery, it being a favorite sport among all classes of people. The professionals who had their shops in the city of Lhasa catering to the officials and others taking interest in the game often came from this valley. During the New Year festivities, many senior officials of the Tibetan Government, including the ministers, had to take part in contests of long-distance shooting. They themselves did not participate in the annual competition but hired men from Phenpo to represent them. Besides attending this event, all junior officials had personally to participate in tests of riding and shooting guns and arrows on horseback. This event took place once in four or five years, depending on the number of junior officials who had entered the government service. The Phenpo archers were reserved to serve them during the entire period of practice and they were looked after lavishly. There was fierce competition among the senior and best performers who all sought excellence in their performance. Usually, the best shooters would reach a distance of 800 yards or more depending on the wind direction. If one was lucky, the wind direction might add several yards. Here, the Phenpo archers were very much involved in supporting their employers. Their closely guarded technique was in balancing the bow and arrow by matching the strength of the bow to the weight of the arrow.

There are two types of bow and arrow. One type is for short distances, to be aimed at a target placed about thirty yards away. A light, hollow, wooden block with small holes opened on the sides is fixed on the head of the arrow, so that when it travels, it makes a whistling sound. Another type of bow and arrow is for long-distance shots. The arrows are very thin with long metal points fixed on the ends. The bow is very stiff and only a man of strength can use the good bows, which can shoot a distance of over two thousand feet.

❀   ❀   ❀

In the family of Khakhor Shi were my grandparents, their three sons, and their daughter. The eldest was a son named Thondup Norbu, the second was Nangang (my father), the third was a son named Phuntsok Wangdu, and the youngest was a daughter, Yangchen Dolkar. Nangang was the first name of my father because he was born on New Year's eve. The last day of each month is called *nangang* in Tibetan. Since the conception of my father, good luck had fallen on his parents and the house prospered; therefore, he was considered to be the source of this luck.

My grandfather died of a sudden illness when my father was five years old. Since my grandmother was left to care for the land and the young children, she experienced much difficulty and hardship. She then married my grandfather's cousin, Lhundup La. Lhundup La was a hot-tempered man who used to beat both mother and children. Soon the elder sister of Lhundup, Somo Nyila, came from Lhasa to live with the family in Phenpo, and after having stayed there for some time, she saw the difficulties in the home. Out of pity for the children, who were harshly treated by their stepfather, she took the three sons to Lhasa to live with her. She lived in an apartment in a mansion named Karma Sharchen, which is in the center of the city. Somo Nyila was a kind and religious woman. She shared her wealth with her relatives and friends, and often distributed food, clothing, and money to the poor of the city. It was the custom for the proud Phenpo Tibetans to visit the major temples in their home town during the religious festivals as well as on the eighth, fifteenth, and the last day of the month. Somo Nyila never forgot her offerings and her visits to the temples in Lhasa City. She brought up the children with kindness, love, and understanding. The children were sent in 1895 to a private school in the city, Phalai Labtra. When Thondup Norbu, the eldest, came of age, she gave him in marriage to one of her friend's daughters, and he left her home. In 1900, a monk official of the Tibetan Government, Khangnyi Jinpa La, who was also a close and faithful friend and family adviser of Somo Nyila, took my father as his pupil. Khangnyi Jinpa La was in charge of Norbu Lingka, the summer palace of the Dalai Lama, and was also one of the older personal attendants of His Holiness the Thirteenth Dalai Lama. A couple of years passed while my father was trained in household work, as well as Tibetan literature and scriptures, and he earned the trust of his master and tutor.

It was on one of these days while my father was in the service of Khangnyi Jinpa La that His Holiness the Thirteenth Dalai Lama came to the house and noticed him. The Dalai Lama was a most observant man, who took care to make routine checks in and around his palace, stables, and compounds. On one such occasion, when he surprised his personal attendants in their quarters, he saw my father and was struck by an unusual air of intelligence in the young boy. After finding out about the background of the boy from Jinpa La, he recruited him as one of his servants. Father was twelve years old when he left Jinpa La's service to join the Dalai Lama's personal staff. He served well in the palace and soon came to have the confidence of the Dalai Lama and the confidence and respect of the other members of the staff as well.

❋   ❋   ❋

In 1890, a treaty was signed by the Governor General of British India and the Manchus defining the boundary between Tibet and Sikkim. Another agreement was signed, known as the Trade Regulations Agreement of 1893, in which the question of increasing trade facilities across the Sikkim-Tibet frontier was introduced. These treaties were regarded as invalid by the Tibetan Government, which never accepted or recognized them, as Tibet was not a member of the signing parties. The British India Government then sought to open direct negotiations with Tibet in pursuit of these two treaties and to clarify her relations with Tibet.

In July of 1903, five British officers, including Captain Frederick O'Connor, arrived at Khampa Dzong with 200 troops as an advance party. This was followed by Younghusband and an additional 400 men. They camped for about three months before returning to Sikkim without gaining a settlement with the Tibetans. Talks remained pending until the second Younghusband expedition, which took place from late 1903 to early 1904. Fighting broke out in Chemi Shongo, where 650 Tibetan troops were killed and 300 men imprisoned by the British. The British advanced through Gyantse and the Kharo and Ghampa Passes to Lhasa.

When the Tibetan Government learned of the arrival of the troops at Ghampa Pass, the Dalai Lama was advised to flee north via Phenpo and Taklung to Reting Monastery, which had been built in 1075 by the famous lama Drom Tonpa. The Dalai Lama fled with a party of about 100 men, Khangnyi Jinpa La among them. Druk Lobsang Rinchen was selected as the new officer in charge of the Norbu Lingka Palace before the Dalai Lama fled north, and my father was left to acquaint the new officer with the daily functions of this place. After a few days at Norbu Lingka working with the new officer, Father left to catch up with the Dalai Lama and his party. He traveled day and night until he reached Reting. After a few days' rest in Reting Monastery, they arrived at Nakchu Dukhang Monastery, where they were well received by the monks. Both the monasteries gave a tremendous reception to His Holiness, confirming their loyalty and providing a great service as well.

These monasteries lay along a route called Changlam, or the Northern Road, leading from southern and central Tibet to northern Tibet, western China, and Mongolia. This route runs along a vast plateau, the highest altitudes reaching 16,500 feet. The plateau is not dry, but rich in grass in the summer season. Because of the natural grazing land, the majority of the nomads of Tibet live in this area. Most of the nomadic families own at least 100 yaks and *dris*, the female yak, and about 1,000 sheep. They also keep horses for riding. The staple foods of these nomads are meat, cheese, butter, and milk. Barley and wheat are also staple foods of Tibet, but it is difficult for the nomads to obtain these products. They are available only when the nomads leave for the lower lands during the severe cold of winter, when they take their loads of yak tails and yak and sheep wool to trade for grain, tea, cotton, needles, and thread. The wool is bought by Tibetan merchants and exported to India by mule. Wool was one of Tibet's largest exports at that time.

Travelers have to carry their own tents or lodge in one of the nomads' tents overnight because no houses exist. In winter it is so cold that after a night's rest, the tents which need to be packed that morning for another day's journey are stiff from the cold and must be heated before they can be folded and packed. Animals and people have difficulty keeping the frost off their noses in the early morning air, and at this high altitude they find it hard to breathe. It is a wonder that so many nomads and their flocks can get acclimatized and survive through this long hard winter, as they roam in search of dry grass. When these nomads meet with a blizzard—these storms are quite common during wintertime—men and animals perish in large numbers.

The plateau of Changthang is full of animals such as wild ass, deer, gazelle, wild sheep, and numerous *dong* and *drelmo*. The *dong* is of the yak family, but wild and twice the size of a yak or a big bull. The length of its horn may measure about four feet, and have a circumference of eight inches. The nomads use the horns of this animal to carry drinking water. The *dongs* travel in herds, but the male *dong* stays alone; and it is most dangerous for anyone to disturb this animal. A *dong* cannot be killed with just a few shots of a rifle, and it is only when its blood is drained and the animal is weak from exhaustion that a person can go near it. The flesh of this animal is rather tough, and people do not rate it as good meat. The heart of a *dong* is very rare and is used in Tibet as a heart medicine. Insomnia is controlled by the blood of this heart; people take a drop or two of the blood in their *chang*, the local barley beer.

The *drelmo* is a most unusual animal, like the *dong*, and is only found in Tibet. This animal is like a bear and lives in holes made in mounds. Its fur is four to eight inches in length. Stories are told of two related species of the *drelmo*. One is called *midrel* ("human *drelmo*") and the other, *chudrel* ("water *drelmo*"). It is told that at times a *midrel* would come to steal a human child in order to mother it, or a male *midrel* would steal a young girl and keep her. I have never seen a *midrel* myself, but have been warned

on many occasions to take care during journeys through uninhabited regions of the country.

A part of this northern route along the Changthang lies along
a salt marsh. Miles and miles of the road are covered with salt,
which is sometimes heaped up to form a small rock. This salt is
rich in quality and free for the taking. The nomads collect this
salt in woolen bags and bring them to the villages and towns to
trade for the goods they require. This part of Tibet is rich in oil,
gold, minerals, and coal. Travelers come across these natural
products, but no one has ever sought for more than what they
find on their journey.

❀   ❀   ❀

When the Dalai Lama and his party reached Tangla Pass, the
highest area on the Changlam, an unusual thunderstorm took
place. They said among themselves that the protective deities of
the country were disturbed. His Holiness was then requested to
pray. Finally the weather became calm, and no one was harmed
by the storm.

When they reached the area of Shokhul, they encountered a
group of 500 bandits. Bandits are common on the Changlam and
many travelers have lost their goods and lives under surprise
attack. These men were on horseback and it is believed that the
Dalai Lama's party decided to wait for the bandits to come up to
them. When they were approached, they shouted that the Dalai
Lama was amongst their group. The moment they heard the name
"Dalai Lama," the bandits disarmed themselves, and came forward to receive the blessings of the Holy One.

At one point during their night, the party was in need of a
consultation with the Nechung Oracle to determine how to pro-
ceed. Often oracles are consulted in difficult situations, as they
can advise the best course of action. Only at this time did the
party realize that the medium had been left behind, and all they
had was the *tadung* for protection. The *tadung* was the Oracle's
staff, a power-object with colorful banners attached to the top.
One among the attendants suggested trying to use a clean, young
man, together with the *tadung* to invoke the spirit. My father was

selected for this attempt. When the invocation prayers were chanted, Father was not able to go into trance, but instead his right hand, holding the *tadung*, began to shake uncontrollably. From the movements of the *tadung* the group was able to decipher the advice being offered and proceeded accordingly.

The oracles are highly placed spirits which may haunt their previous dwellings or places nearby. When called by the chanting of lamas, the spirit comes round and takes possession of a person who has been previously selected as the medium. When the spirit attains full possession of the man, he then predicts future events.

The topmost oracle of Tibet is the Nechung Oracle, the state protector, and second to him is the Gadong. The two lamas who are able to be possessed by these elite spirits are given high titles. The mediums for both these oracles managed to escape from Tibet during the Lhasa revolt of 1959 and are now with the present Dalai Lama, the fourteenth, in Dharamsala, India.

After traveling for about three weeks in uninhabited land, His Holiness reached the village of Kulu Paktse. A night was spent in this village in order to give their horses a rest after the long and strenuous journey. They then left for Yongdon Palsi Monastery on camel. A week was spent here, and the Grand Lama, Khalkha Jetsun of Urga, sent his personal representatives to welcome and pay his respects to the Dalai Lama. A certain misunderstanding came about when the haughty manner of the interpreter offended the Mongols. It seems that while trying to control the mad rush to see His Holiness, the interpreter referred to one of the representatives as an "animal." Afterwards, when His Holiness arrived at Urga, a poor reception was given for him and his party.

A few days later, the Grand Lama of Mongolia, Jetsun Dhampa, was seen coming towards the monastery and, with much excitement, preparation was made to receive him. But when the Grand Lama approached, accompanied by his wife, Tsakhang Tari, a few servants, and his dogs, he barged in and entered the Dalai Lama's private room without greeting anyone. After joking amongst themselves in their own language and hitting each other in childish play, the party immediately left without even a greeting to the Tibetans, leaving the Dalai Lama and his attendants perplexed. With the echoes of the barking dogs, the Grand Lama and his party disappeared.

Upon the arrival of His Holiness in Urga, Mongols from every part of the country came to receive his blessings, bringing many gifts for him. The news of the Holy One's arrival was spread far and wide. Tens of thousands of people came to see the Dalai Lama from all areas of Mongolia and from Siberia. His popularity was deeply resented by the Grand Lama, who, because of it, became extremely jealous of the Dalai Lama.

Early one morning, the Grand Lama and five of his staff dressed up as Chinese opera characters. Old men in different colored robes, with beards matching the color of their costumes and armed with rifles, approached Gaden Monastery, where the Dalai Lama was staying. Instead of making the clockwise circuit around the monastery in Buddhist fashion, they walked the other way round in order to offend the Buddhists, even though the Grand Lama was a Buddhist himself. After the walk, they barged into the audience hall of the monastery. The Grand Lama wanted to know why His Holiness was using a throne when he was receiving guests in public audience. After making his complaints to the monks of the monastery, he ordered the throne to be pulled down and thrown out, and then left the monastery.

On another occasion, the Grand Lama, Jetsun Dhampa, invited the Dalai Lama and his party to his palace. His Holiness received the invitation with courtesy and arrived at the palace with a couple of his personal servants, including my father. The Dalai Lama was climbing up the stairs in the palace when he came across an image of Jey Tsongkapa, the Reformer, the founder of the Gelugpa sect of Buddhism in Tibet, conspicuously placed at the top of the staircase. The odd placement of this holy image was an insult to the head of a country whose religion was Buddhism. A statue of Jey Tsongkapa should be carefully kept inside a *lhakhang*, a shrine room especially designated to house such images.

Immediately after seeing the image on the staircase, the Dalai Lama was taken for a tour of the palace, and one of the first stops was the Grand Lama's personal bedroom. Here he was shown the place where the Grand Lama slept with his wife. This situation was a real breach of cultural protocol and a great embarrassment to His Holiness. He was then shown the rooms displaying the Grand Lama's treasures, and particularly a room where hundreds of watches from his collection were on view: this room was filled with the chimes and ticking of clocks. When the tour came to an end and most of the rooms had been shown, he led His Holiness and his attendants through a narrow corridor into a small room where, to the surprise of the visitors, they saw two monks in chains with their heads enclosed in iron grilles. The Grand Lama explained that he had caught these two monks drinking in a local wine house that he had inspected the night before, and he had brought them there to punish them for their misdeeds. Monks are, of course, forbidden to have any alcoholic drinks.

In the meantime, the Dalai Lama received the good news of the settlement between Tibet and the British Government at Lhasa. A convention was drawn up and the British forces left Lhasa but established a Trade Agent at Gyantse with a token force of seventy-five sepoys to guard the trade mart. Similar agents were also posted at Yatung, the small border town between Tibet and India, and at Gartok in Western Tibet.

Being young and intelligent, Father had learned to speak Mongolian quite well during his long stay at Urga and proved to be most useful as an interpreter between the Mongols and His Holiness. Later, His Holiness also learned the language. A Japanese monk, Tokan Tada, who stayed at Sera Monastery in Lhasa, wrote in his book, *The Thirteenth Dalai Lama*: "The Dalai Lama was facile in speaking Mongolian. Minister Tsarong, too, could speak Mongolian very well, so that often they talked in Mongolian about important affairs of State."

News of the Russian defeat in the Russo-Japanese war reached Urga; several thousand had lost their lives in battle. A rumor was spread that the Japanese were coming to invade the city. As revolutionary uprisings were breaking out in Russia, the atmosphere was tense in the Mongol capital. It was then, in the seventh month of the Tibetan calendar in the year 1905, that the Dalai Lama and his party left Urga without even a farewell reception from the Grand Lama.

Father then traveled with His Holiness's party to several places in Inner and Outer Mongolia. During His Holiness's stay at Zayenkhurel, he met the Amban (Chinese Representative), and the Russian Consul. The meetings were cordial. Later, the Russian Minister to China, sent by Tsar Nicholas, came and immediately upon his arrival called on His Holiness. On behalf of the Russian emperor, he offered the assistance of his country. At that time, the Empress Dowager also sent a representative from Peking to pay her respects to His Holiness.

In 1906, the Dalai Lama was invited by Khandro Chin Wang to give Dharma teachings at his monastery. The party was given a grand reception and Father wrote in his journal that, "an unimaginably good sermon was delivered by His Holiness." It was during this time that Father underwent Russian military training for a couple of months. His Holiness continued his travels and was invited by several district chiefs to come and give blessings and teachings. In 1907, he went to Senoyong and again sermons were given which truly touched those in attendance. After Senoyong, Lama Gegun invited him to his monastery and there a great number of people gathered—from small children to the very old—all feeling profound respect for His Holiness.

Altogether His Holiness spent one and a half years in Mongolia on pilgrimage. During that time, he was very reserved and well-disciplined. People were impressed with his dignified manner. Just at the sight of him they felt great respect. He received many people, ordained many new monks in the Buddhist faith, and gave memorable Dharma teachings in the towns and villages through which he traveled.

Towards the end of 1908, in the Tibetan year of the Earth Monkey, the Dalai Lama's party reached the Koko Nor area, and stayed in Kumbum Monastery. Kumbum is the birthplace of Tsongkapa, the founder of the Gelugpa sect of Tibetan Buddhism. Tsongkapa was born in the year 1357, near a sandalwood tree. A small temple existed at that time, and later the Third Dalai Lama built the "Monastery of a Hundred Thousand Images," or Kumbum Monastery, at the site. At the time of His Holiness the Thirteenth Dalai Lama's visit to this monastery, there were about 5,000 monks in residence. These monks were mostly from the

Koko Nor area and elsewhere in Amdo Province, in the eastern domain of Tibet and Mongolia. His Holiness the Fourteenth Dalai Lama was also born in this area. The images in this monastery are countless and priceless. Tibetans would not miss visiting this monastery on pilgrimage when traveling in this region.

While His Holiness was residing in Kumbum after leaving Urga and Inner Mongolia, he officially gave my father the title of Leytsen, the fifth rank in the Tibetan Government. There are seven ranks in the governmental system, the Dalai Lama holding the highest (first) rank. Father had also been given the name Chen-tsel, which was only used when referring to the rare few who were designated as close associates. The literal translation of this name is "clear eyes," and it means "as seen through the clear eyes of His Holiness." Later on it became a nickname for Father; everyone called him Chen-tsel. Many people have since misinterpreted this name, regarding the "clear eyes" to be those of Tsarong. However, this name actually referred to the eyes of the Dalai Lama, which were able to clearly perceive who were to be the trusted favorites.

It was during this period that His Holiness was invited to visit China. He accepted in order to maintain friendly relations with the Chinese. His Holiness and his party left for Peking through Sian Fu towards the end of 1907, spending some time visiting Buddhist monasteries en route. In Wu Tai Shan in the Shansi Province, the American diplomat in China, William W. Rockhill, called on the party. This was the first official contact between Tibet and the United States of America.

When His Holiness the Dalai Lama arrived in Peking in September of 1908, he was received by the Manchu Government in a befitting ceremony. A guard of honor presented arms; and, along with a multitude of people, including officers, monks, and musicians, His Holiness was taken in procession to his place of residence.

2 Conflict with China

At the railway station, a host of foreigners also came to watch the arrival of the Dalai Lama, and many among them took photographs. My father viewed these photographers with interest—he later became quite good at taking photographs himself. When he returned to Tibet with His Holiness, he brought many cameras and photographic supplies. Some of these cameras were very big and had beautifully polished wooden cases. Later, in Lhasa, Tsarong Wangchuk Gyalpo, my maternal grandfather, would instruct him in photography.

After a few days, His Holiness was received by the Emperor and Empress Dowager, Tzsu Hsi. A fitting reception was given to the Dalai Lama, which my father also attended. Later he wrote in his diary:

> His Holiness and his entourage were given a grand reception by the Emperor; lavish food was laid on the table, and musicians played flutes and other instruments. While we were served, wrestlers performed in front of the party. Tehlun Solje, who was the Panchen Lama's Master of Tea, was sitting next to me. He said that this was a great opportunity: the pleasure of having dinner with the Emperor, and it would be fitting for me to pick up a momo and put it in my pocket to take home. I did this, and on our return to the monastery, Tehlun Solje, Rampa Tsepong, and others asked me to give them each a small piece of the momo, which I divided until it was finished. They considered this very auspicious.

His Holiness then began to meet with the British, Japanese, and other foreign representatives stationed at Peking. These were the first direct connections made by the Dalai Lama with foreign dignitaries. My father was fortunate to be present on every

occasion. Although he was a young man, he became a very useful and trusted assistant to His Holiness.

In November 1908, while His Holiness was still in Peking, the
Emperor of China passed away, and the very next day, the Empress Dowager died. His Holiness visited many Buddhist
temples and offered prayers for the departed souls.

After a long stay in Peking, His Holiness and his party left
without making much progress in their discussions with the Chinese Government. At the time, China was experiencing much
internal conflict amongst feuding warlords. His Holiness had
also received disturbing news from Lhasa about Chinese activities in Tibet itself. The Chinese were beginning to invade Tibetan
territory, entering monasteries and destroying precious artifacts,
stealing, and even killing, like lawless bandits. It seemed that
once the Empress Dowager passed away, the relationship with
the Chinese Government began to deteriorate. With feelings of
suspicion, the party left Peking for Tibet.

On the way, His Holiness halted again at Kumbum Monastery, where he spent quite a long time before continuing on to
the capital. During this time, unsettling reports continued to arrive from Lhasa along with requests that he should return quickly
due to the breaking down of relations with the Chinese. Soon,
His Holiness and his party set out for Lhasa, and on their arrival
at Nagchuka, they were received by the Panchen Lama, the
Amban, and other Tibetan officials. The officials' second welcoming party met him at Reting, which is about three days' horseback journey from Lhasa. The third and final party, which
included the three Joint Prime Ministers, the Cabinet Ministers,
and others, came to receive the Dalai Lama at a distance of about
three miles from the capital. The next day, November 9, 1909, His
Holiness entered the city in a grand procession, and the whole
city was filled with joy. The people of Tibet presented the Dalai
Lama with a great gold seal, a mark confirming him as their
ruler and as supreme head of the Church.

During my father's stay in Mongolia and China he had met
many foreigners and was able to pick up a few different languages which later became quite useful. While in China, he also
had the opportunity to make extensive tours of neighboring

countries. He traveled to Chita in Russia, and Harbin, Mukden, and Port Arthur in Manchuria. His visits and contacts with foreigners widened his knowledge of the outside world, and he was able to procure modern cameras, watches, and other novelties for His Holiness. He also acquired instruments such as a protractor and a theodolite which were useful later for surveying work.

As previously mentioned, he met the American diplomat William W. Rockhill at Wu Tai Shan in Shansi Province, when he was traveling with His Holiness on their way to Peking. Later, when he reached Tibet, he exchanged letters with Mr. Rockhill and received an excellent gift of a pair of automatic pistols with gold inlay, encased in a beautiful, polished wooden case embellished with my father's monogram. He treasured them, and later gave them to me. I kept them and maintained them in their original condition until I left Tibet in 1957. I believe my father got hold of them again, and they must have fallen into the hands of the Chinese Communists when he was arrested in March, 1959.

News from the border was constantly worrying His Holiness and the ministers. Special messengers arrived with reports, and with each new development it became clearer that the situation was going from bad to worse. When the news came that a strong force of mounted Chinese advance troops and cavalry were approaching along the Kyichu River in Lhasa, His Holiness summoned the National Assembly. It was then decided that for the safety of His Holiness, he should move to Dromo along with the ministers.

It was early 1910, on the second day of the Tibetan New Year—which is considered a more important day than the New Year's day itself—when the Chinese troops entered the Holy City. This day is called the "King's New Year"; everybody was celebrating and in a festive mood when the soldiers arrived behaving like wild bandits. They fired their rifles at the unsuspecting Tibetans and many were wounded and killed.

Earlier, my father had been ordered to the front with a small force of the Dalai Lama's guards in response to reports of the oncoming Chinese. However, before crossing the river, he was told to retreat at once because it would be futile for such a small force to face the Chinese advance. By evening, Father returned to the Norbu Lingka with the detachment. That same night, His Holiness with his ministers and other attendants left silently, crossing the Kyichu River at Ramagang Ferry. This is the same river crossing that His Holiness the Fourteenth Dalai Lama would use for his escape to India in 1959.

Father followed His Holiness on the main road with his men, and having reached the town of Chushul, he planned to defend it against the Chinese pursuing force. The townspeople requested him not to stay there as the Chinese were sure to destroy the place and kill many people. They asked him to move to Chaksam Ferry, assuring him that they would use all possible means to support him. The Chaksam Ferry crossing is about four miles from Chushul. It is a desolate, empty place except for a small monastery on the far side of the river. *Chaksam* means "iron bridge," named for an innovative suspension bridge that was built there more than five hundred years ago by the great saint Thang Tong Gyalpo. Thang Tong Gyalpo is revered by Tibetans for his masterful accomplishments in drama, song, architecture, medicine, and religion. He was a great innovator and it is said that he built 108 iron suspension bridges throughout Tibet and Bhutan. Passing through Chaksam in my school days, I remember seeing the two long iron chains, which were all that remained of the bridge. The only crossing possible then was by ferry.

It was at Chaksam that Father decided to oppose the Chinese forces. Upon arrival, he ordered his force of sixty-seven men to cross by ferry and pull all the boats up on their side of the Brahmaputra. Strict orders were issued to the boatmen not to send any boats to the other side of the river unless they received permission to do so. They waited impatiently; there was no sign of the Chinese approaching the riverside. An icy wind was blowing along the river, and it was pitch dark when a messenger reached the other side of the river with a warning that the Chinese had reached Chushul. The man shouted that there were about 300 Chinese mounted troops, and when they had learned that all boats had been withdrawn to the Tibetan side, they began pulling down beams and window frames from some houses and making rafts. The man added, at the top of his voice, that the Chinese would be here if not by early dawn, definitely before sunrise.

The good news was also received by my father that His Holiness and his party had safely crossed the Gonkar Ferry, and, after withdrawing the boats, the party was proceeding to Samding Monastery, where they intended to halt for a good rest. Samding is the seat of Dorje Phagmo, the highest female incarnation in Tibet, who is abbess of the monastery there. My father immediately sent an urgent message to Samding advising them that the Chinese had already reached Chushul. He assured those ahead that he would make every effort to put up a stiff resistance, but, to be on the safe side, His Holiness should leave immediately. He then inspected his troops, who were deployed along the hillocks, and retired with some of his lieutenants to the Chaksam monastery, which is situated at the mouth of the river.

My father was by then very tired and fell asleep immediately. At early dawn he was awakened by a strange dream, a vision of a woman from Tsang Province, with full headdress, who slapped him hard. He actually felt it painfully, and when he rose, he heard some people talking in Chinese below the building. Immediately he called his men and rushed through the back door to the hillside. Some gunfire was exchanged at this point, but there were no casualties on either side. This I later learned from both my father and a Chinese man named Du Gen, who led a group of seven Chinese soldiers. These seven were an advance party that had already crossed the river on a raft. Du Gen would later side with my father when he was fighting the Chinese in Lhasa.

At the gray light of dawn, the Chinese were in three groups preparing for their crossing. A moment later, there was heavy fire from the Chinese side, but the Tibetans remained quiet and under cover. The great advantage the Tibetans had was that their position was on a hillock with many boulders, but the Chinese side of the river was just a sandy, flat beach. Strict orders were given not to fire a single shot on the beach except to return the fire given by Du Gen and his men. It was also made clear that the first shot would be fired by my father as a signal to his men. At sunrise, the Chinese gunfire had subsided considerably, and a little later the Chinese soldiers began to float their rafts on the river. Some also used wooden beams to cross the water. At this point my father gave the signal, and it was the Tibetans' turn to go into action. The Chinese troops were fully exposed on the riverside and they scattered wildly in all directions, some falling from their horses. Within a short period the battle was over, leaving about 170 Chinese and many horses dead on the beach. The casualties on the Tibetan side were eleven men and five horses. My father, seeing that there was no point in fighting the Chinese further with his small force, and having no ammunition in reserve, dispersed all his men, and with two servants he followed after His Holiness.

That same night, after riding about thirty miles, my father reached Nagartse. He entered a house and when he asked for food and shelter, it was refused. He then found another house, where he was received kindly by a poor family. This hospitality was a great help to my father in his hour of need. Upon his departure, he left ten *sang*, which was quite a sum in those days. He rested about three hours, and continued his journey. In order to avoid the Chinese, he took a shorter route which led him to Khangmar, bypassing the town of Gyantse. Upon reaching Khangmar, he learned that the British Trade Agent at Gyantse, Mr. James Weir, was staying at the British rest house. He met Mr. Weir, who informed him that the Dalai Lama had safely reached Phari, and that the Chinese garrison at Gyantse had dispatched mounted troops who would be reaching Khangmar shortly. He advised him not to follow the main route as it would be highly dangerous now. My father then disguised himself as a telegraph linesman and left for Phari riding along the Chomo Lhari mountain range. It was deep into winter and snow had started falling throughout the day and night. The icy winds pierced him, and from time to time he had to walk briskly to keep himself warm.

He reached Phari in the late afternoon of the following day, and while resting at the house of the Genpo (sheriff), news of the arrival of the Chinese troops and their enquiry about him was reported to my father. It was now pitch dark, and when the Chinese reached the main gate, he immediately slipped through the back window and jumped to a pile of refuse accumulated at the back of the house. He then ran directly to the British rest house at Phari and knocked on the door. Outside, he waited anxiously, and it took some time before the door was opened.

A man with an oil lamp opened the door. My father was panting, and as he was explaining his desperate situation , two other men came from inside. As he took a step to enter, he accidentally fired his loaded Mauser pistol. The shot hit a lamp and caused great confusion. He tried his best to explain what had happened. After some time, the officer in charge of the telegraph line, Mr. Rosemeyer, came out from his room into the courtyard to settle the commotion. Father was well looked after there. He rested a couple of hours, and then Mr. Rosemeyer arranged for a man to accompany him onward. They left for Dromo by making a detour, and reached a hill thickly covered with pine trees below which the residence of the British Trade Agent, Mr. David Macdonald, was located. They waited until dusk, and then started descending. He reached the residence during the night and rested there for two days.

His escape route had been discussed further by his friends, and on the second morning they decided to disguise Father as a post-carrier and send him to the border along with the regular runners. By that time, fresh Chinese troops had already reached Dromo and were even beyond the town area. It was early in the morning when he headed with another post-carrier towards the Jelep La Pass. These carriers usually walk fast and sometimes double march; they are then replaced after every five miles with a fresh man. Carriers are armed with spears to which small bells are attached, so that when they run, the noise of the bells alerts those ahead of their approach and signals to clear the road. My father was unable to keep up with the carrier, as he was near exhaustion from having to march straight through without rest. So he sent his mail bag and spear on with his partner and slowly started to walk up the pass.

The snow was falling continually, and about one mile below Langra, where there was a small detachment of Chinese guards, he saw a distant fire from which it looked as though some travelers were resting for the night in a rocky cave. It was a Tibetan couple on their way to Kalimpong, and they helped him by offering food and bedding. The man went up to Langra to see whether the Chinese sentry was on the alert or not. He soon came back and reported that the Chinese officers were lying in bed smoking opium, and the sentry would also go into the house after some time, so he told my father to rest and warm himself till then. About midnight, the man again came with my father up to Langra, and, leaving Father a little behind, he spied upon them and helped my father cross safely. Later, my father told me that at Langra he had to pass directly between the Chinese troops, who were sleeping in the wooden houses erected on both sides of the road.

It was still snowing when he left his helpful friend, having paid him a hundred *sang* for his assistance. Fortunately, the snow stopped and there was no sharp wind. The thought that this was his last march to free himself brought great encouragement to keep on walking. It was also better to climb the pass while it was not snowing and avoid the sharp, piercing wind of the late dawn. He managed to cross the treacherous pass before sunrise, and it brought a great sense of relief. Father felt exhausted, but was now able to relax, having crossed the danger zone. Moreover, he was overjoyed when he met the Dalai Lama's men with their mules, who came to fetch him. The Chinese in Tibet had offered a handsome price for the head of my father and alerted all their checkposts throughout Tibet. Meanwhile, the Dalai Lama had arrived in Kalimpong, and he was well received by the Raja Ugyen Dorji of Bhutan. The Dalai Lama stayed at the government rest house for a few days, during which time an endless stream of visitors came to the house to receive his blessing.

Father soon reached Darjeeling, where His Holiness was then staying at the Hotel Drum-Druid, on the Chowrasta Mall. His Holiness and his entourage received my father with great joy, and from then on he was an important member of the Dalai Lama's court.

From there, Father accompanied His Holiness when he was invited to meet the Viceroy in Calcutta. The party left Darjeeling in the middle of March; the weather was already beginning to get warm. After coming from such a cold country, His Holiness and his attendants found the heat uncomfortable, and they hoped to make the return trip to Darjeeling soon. On the day of His Holiness's arrival in Calcutta, a seventeen-gun salute was fired in his honor, and the party was driven in carriages to Hastings House, where he was the guest of the government.

His Holiness then called on the Viceroy, who later made a return call at Hastings House. The Dalai Lama met the Viceroy and expressed his gratitude for the kind hospitality extended to him, and then related the account of his escape from the Chinese. He told them of the great hardships he had had to face, being constantly threatened by the Chinese troops who had pursued him. He added that the Chinese had adopted a hostile attitude towards him and had shown designs to annex the whole of Tibet. Further discussions took place through Mr. Charles Bell, who was then the British Political Officer in Sikkim.

Despite the heat in Calcutta, His Holiness and party visited the zoo and the museum. However, he soon left for Darjeeling, and many members of the party welcomed the day, for the temperature was becoming increasingly hot. The weather in Darjeeling provided much relief from the hot plains of India. The party did not stay at their previous hotel, but instead settled at Hillside Kuti, a house a short distance away from the town on the Lebong Cart Road. Today it is occupied by the Tibetan Refugee Self-Help Center, a handicraft center which was established in 1960 by the Fourteenth Dalai Lama's sister-in-law.

Throughout the summer months His Holiness remained in Darjeeling. It was during these months that news coming from Tibet turned from bad to worse. The Chinese had seized all of His Holiness's personal belongings that had not yet reached Lhasa from his last trip to China and Mongolia. The Tibetan Government's treasury was emptied, and the armory was looted. All the Dalai Lama's personal belongings were also removed by the Chinese from these various places.

Father made two trips to Calcutta during the year to make purchases for His Holiness. He had already picked up a few words of English and Hindustani and was starting to get better acquainted with the country. During the winter, he again accompanied His Holiness when the latter visited several Buddhist centers around India.

3 War Hero

One morning, His Holiness was going around the *stupas* at Benares, when he stopped at a certain place where a very old pile of earth resembling an ancient damaged *stupa* was being pulled down by some workmen. He saw that the work was being supervised by a British officer and that he was taking out some bits and pieces from a pot which lay on a table nearby. When His Holiness saw this, he told my father that according to religious books many relics of the Lord Buddha were distributed to various sacred places, and he was quite sure that this was one of them; my father was to obtain some if possible. So Father went over to the guard standing near a table on which the small relics had been placed with great care. He did not know how much money he had in his pocket; but he showed a handful to the man, who then exchanged it for a handful of bone-like objects, without being seen by the British officer. He then gave these to His Holiness, who was immensely pleased with them and took them to his residence. Later a small quantity was given to my father, who treasured the precious relics and took them back to Tibet. Many years later, when my father built his new house on the outskirts of Lhasa, he placed the relics inside images of the three great religious kings which were housed in the main family *lhakhang* (chapel).

Eventually the Dalai Lama and his entourage returned to Darjeeling. Every day there were people from the countryside who came to receive the blessings of the Holy One. Day after day they made prayers for a speedy return to their own country. These prayers were conducted by His Holiness. He was assisted by the lamas who were with him to serve him on such religious occasions.

One day, His Holiness told Father that he wished to visit Kurseong, a town about eighteen miles from Darjeeling, to see a special Buddhist temple. This temple, according to his knowledge and belief, was an important place because it was one of the seats of the Oracle Gyalchen Shungden. The Dalai Lama visited the temple with Father and, pointing to a large tree at the back of the temple, said that the spirit of Gyalchen Shungden often dwelled at this spot. Later in 1958, when Father visited Darjeeling, he wanted to go to Kurseong, to visit the temple again. I told him I did not know where it was and that I had never heard of such a temple, but he insisted and suggested we inquire at the Tibetan community there. Upon our arrival, one of the Tibetan shopkeepers told us that the temple was just ahead and pointed out the way. We reached the place and offered scarves and prayers. He then took me around to the backyard where there was a very old tree about ten feet in diameter. The trunk was painted with red and white horizontal stripes. At the trunk's base, the ground was raised to form a platform on which incense and other offerings were made. He told me that this was the spot where the spirit of Gyalchen Shungden often dwelled. He added that the spirit also haunted other places in Tibet and elsewhere.

Earlier during His Holiness's exile in Mongolia in 1904, my father had been sent for Russian military training. Again, while with the Dalai Lama's party in Darjeeling, he was sent for military training, this time to the British Army headquarters at Lebong, just outside the center of Darjeeling. As advised by friends, His Holiness made arrangements for Father to enter St. Joseph's College.

When the news of the revolution in China reached the Holy City, antigovernment groups among the Chinese mutinied. They attacked the Amban's residence and arrested him. Encouraged by the favorable situation, the Tibetans became more bold against the Chinese and later openly attacked them. Full-scale fighting then took place between the two forces. The city was divided into two zones: the northern part held by the Tibetans, and the southern by the Chinese. At this time, letters passed freely between the Dalai Lama in India and the Tibetan authorities in Lhasa.

Although Father was preparing to go to college (his school uniforms had already been ordered), when the news of the Chinese revolution and the increasing Tibetan hostility against the Chinese in Tibet reached His Holiness, the Dalai Lama thought that it might be a good idea to send my father back to Lhasa so he could begin to secretly organize a resistance force against the Chinese. It was about this time that the Dalai Lama had a dream, which he later wrote down. He dreamt that he and my father were walking on Gaden Khangsar Street in Lhasa and as they walked, many fierce-looking monkeys appeared in their way. Some were in the middle of the street and others were standing near shop windows about to attack them. Dasang Damdul (the name used for Father by His Holiness) fearlessly attacked the monkeys outright and cleared a way to safety. His Holiness said that this dream indicated a future victory, that Dasang Damdul had the fortunate opportunity to drive the Chinese out of Tibet, and that he should undertake the task immediately.

My father agreed at once and asked His Holiness his advice on the best way to enter Tibet. His Holiness made a fervent prayer and waited for a dream that would indicate the answer. A dream came showing that the preferred entry route was through Ghampa Dzong. He also advised him to perform certain prayers before leaving Darjeeling. All the prayers were performed by His Holiness and the monks in his service at Patapur, better known as Hillside Kuti, his personal residence.

Several months later, His Holiness and his party moved to Kalimpong and stayed at the new house of Kazi Ugyen Dorji, a highly respected Bhutanese Liaison Officer, who built it especially as a residence for His Holiness. The house was called Mingyur Ngongei Phodrang, meaning, "The Indestructible Palace of Delight," and it had a golden top on the roof. In Kalimpong it was commonly known as "Bhutan House." Kazi Dorji and members of his family were very much devoted to His Holiness and received the guests in a fitting manner, which immensely pleased His Holiness and his followers. The room the Dalai Lama occupied can be seen today as it was then. Once when the Queen Mother of Bhutan was visiting Bhutan House, my wife and I were there at a lunch, and she took us to the Dalai Lama's room, which has now become the chapel of the house where all religious functions are held. As we had done previously on many occasions, we sought the blessings of the throne and other priceless images which the Dalai Lama had left there for blessings and remembrances. Besides the throne, the Dalai Lama left his clothes and brocade coverings; even his slippers were left—all maintained in their original condition. The Queen Mother showed us a roll of yellow silk on which a passage in very fine Tibetan script was written. It stated that a title of fourth rank was conferred on the son of Kazi Ugyen Dorji, Sonam Tobgyal, for their family's invaluable service and devotion.

Before my father's departure for Tibet, His Holiness had conferred on him the title of Chida, or Commander General, with credentials giving him wide power to exercise his authority in the effort to subdue the Chinese forces in Tibet. He soon set out, passing through Sikkim and Ghampa Dzong, and reached Gaden Chokhor Monastery, which was about two days' horseback journey from Shigatse. It was a very remote place, and in those days one would have found it difficult to detect any activity of a secret nature going on there. The monastery's inhabitants were exceptionally loyal to the Tibetan Government; it was believed that arms and ammunition were kept in their custody. Even in later years, the Tibetan Government may have stored arms and ammunition at that monastery, because when the Khampas were fighting against the Chinese troops in 1957, a group of Khampas went there to fetch arms. It was at Gaden Chokhor that my father recruited volunteers to fight the Chinese. When the number was to his satisfaction, he led them towards the town of Shigatse, where the *dzong* (fort) was held by the Chinese. The Tibetans, while trying to besiege the fort, had already lost many lives. When my father arrived, the Tibetan forces were much strengthened, and fresh attacks were made. The fighting lasted for five consecutive days under his command, after which the fort was finally surrounded. It took a further twenty-one days to get the Chinese to surrender, and they did so only when their food supply was exhausted.

Father then pushed on towards Nadong, where the Chinese surrendered after putting up some resistance. He was then free to move to Gyantse, but at this stage he realized his presence in Lhasa was more important, so he left for the city. He entered Lhasa at night and arrived at the house of Phunkhang, where he established his headquarters. As mentioned previously, the southern portion of Lhasa City was held by the Chinese and the northern by the Tibetans. In the northern outskirts of the city at Drapshi, only about a mile away, the Chinese had one of their military establishments. Father's first action in Lhasa was the battle for Drapshi.

He planned to attack this position and join forces with the monastery of Sera, which was facing the Chinese from further north. In order to do this, he had to make a piercing attack at Ramochey, which was the only obstacle between the Tibetan forces in the main city and those at Drapshi. He now had many more brave soldiers with him, and the attack was made with two prongs. Much of the fighting was hand-to-hand because in this part of the city the buildings were very close. When the Tibetans got near enough to the buildings, most of them climbed to the rooftops, and moving from one roof to another, they made surprise attacks on the Chinese who were inside. They feared the hand grenades which were used frequently by the Chinese. Within two days, the Chinese were driven out of Ramochey, and the way was clear for the next attack on the main headquarters at Drapshi. Casualties on both sides were few.

My father's next plan was to attack the Chinese headquarters at Drapshi. Along with three hundred men and a reserve of another three hundred, Father marched out of the town in the early dawn and was able to take cover in Shongka Lingka, a spot about half a mile from the Chinese headquarters well covered by trees and shrubs.

At sunrise, the advance party was sent in to face the Chinese fire, but it did not succeed in getting near them. Repeated attempts were made, but the Tibetans finally had to withdraw to their former position. In the late afternoon, the Chinese began to use heavy artillery against the Tibetan position, following it with an infantry attack. My father lost many of his good men and had to retreat to the town at dusk. The day's effort was disappointing, but he had had his first experience of the Chinese strength. He was unable to approach the Chinese from Lhasa and the plan was abandoned.

During the next few days, plans were made to contact Sera Monastery by outflanking the Chinese in secret moves by small groups. This was achieved, and Father and his men were able to join the Sera monks. The monks had been assisted by a small group of Khampas who were harassing the Chinese from time to time.

The position held by the Tibetans was well covered by very long sand dunes. Upon arrival, Father discussed their battle plans with the leaders. He had seen a Chinese guard standing on the gate roof, and the monks explained that he was the most devilish one of the lot. The next morning, Father pushed his rifle slowly between two blocks of earth he had placed there the night before, and took aim at the guard who was standing with his rifle. He shot him, and when the men saw him drop, they rushed towards the gate and entered it. For a long time there were shouts and a great commotion inside the building. The Chinese were overrun by the Tibetans, and about two hundred Chinese were slain or wounded, mostly by swords.

The battle was won by the Tibetans, and what was left of the Chinese garrison escaped to the east of Lhasa. They eventually fortified themselves in Chabzing Lingka, a park with many trees about two miles east of the Holy City. There was still scattered fighting that continued throughout the city at various places.

Meanwhile, a serious situation had developed among the Tibetan leaders. At the time of the Dalai Lama's departure from the Holy City, he had appointed Tsemonling Rinpoche as the Regent and Khenche Neushar as his assistant. The ministers at Lhasa were Shapé Tsarong Wangchuk Gyalpo (my maternal grandfather) and Lobsang Triley. Through the instructions of the Dalai Lama, the Regent had appointed two more assistant ministers, Dekyi Lingpa and Khenchung Gyaltsen Phuntsok. The assistant to the Regent, Neushar, and the newly appointed ministers were not in the good books of the Chinese, and were largely ignored by them. Shapé Tsarong, however, being more acquainted with diplomatic relations and generally an outgoing, friendly man, did not receive the same treatment. This created a great deal of suspicion around my grandfather, to whom the Chinese seemed to have shown some favor. Ultimately, the result was an unfortunate plot formed against Shapé Tsarong and his followers.

Although Shapé Tsarong was a man trusted by the Dalai Lama who had participated in the signing of the Trade Regulation Agreement between Great Britain, China, and Tibet in 1908 at Calcutta, the current situation had brought him overwhelming criticism. Fate turned against him and while participating at a high-level meeting at the Potala Palace, he was arrested and dragged down the long stone steps. He was beheaded there at the foot of the Potala. As arranged previously, his son was also arrested and was brought to see his father's head before being executed on the same spot. Others executed along with Shapé Tsarong and his son were Karung Tsashagpa, Secretary to the Cabinet Ministers; Phunrabpa, Secretary General; Mondhong, the Treasurer, and a few other officials. Simultaneously, there was also fighting among the Chinese troops, which worked in the favor of the Tibetans on the battle fronts. Many Chinese defected and joined the Tibetans. A group of famous swordsmen recruited from Kongpo were guarding what was left of the Chinese troops, who had fortified themselves at Chapzing Lingka after being driven out of Drapshi by the Tibetans. One day, when my father was making his routine inspection, the swordsmen were about to make a charge at the Chinese barricade. He told me that he had tried to stop them, but they just ran wild and flung themselves on the Chinese barricade. Many were killed, and the rest retreated after their fruitless effort. A few days later they were reinforced by my father's group, and took over the barricade facing only small resistance. At this stage, Father had many Chinese fighting on his side and also had arms and ammunition seized from the Chinese. It was through his skillful influence that he was able to win many Chinese over to the Tibetan cause.

Father then concentrated his main effort in the city of Lhasa itself. His next move was to drive the Chinese out from the monastery of Tengyeling. Tengyeling has an interesting history and it is important to mention it in order to understand the Tibetans' position.

In 1895, His Holiness the Thirteenth Dalai Lama was installed on his throne to assume the temporal and religious authority that comes with his title. Demo Rinpoche, who had been Regent up until that time, then took leave, and it is said he did this rather reluctantly. The next year, in 1896, the Nechung Oracle came to know through divination that a spell had been cast on the Government. Later, Oracle Rago Chenpa produced live scorpions from Pelha Chok, the third story of the Tsuglak Khang where the protector deity Palden Lhamo resides. As a young boy, my father witnessed this, telling me that the Oracle took the scorpions out from under the deity with his bare hands. This was read as an evil omen by the officials, and the Nechung Oracle put a warning out to the monks at Loseling College, as well as the chief monks of Drepung, to be alert. The Dalai Lama became increasingly concerned when one day, in trance before His Holiness, the Nechung Oracle told him that a spell against the spiritual leader was to be found in the boot of Terton Sonam Gyaltsen, someone close to His Holiness at that time. The terton was called and claimed he was given the boots by a tea server from Tengyeling, and, when he began to wear them, he started bleeding from the nose without cause or reason. The boots were brought and opened before all the attendants, and found hidden in between one sole was a small paper which carried a curse on His Holiness.

An enquiry committee was soon formed, and Demo Rinpoche was politely held at the Potala, while the others accused were held in prison. After thorough interrogations, the guilty parties confessed. Demo Rinpoche admitted his intentions to hold onto the Regency, but as the much-respected Abbot of Tengyeling Monastery, his punishment was less severe. He was ordered to occupy a separate house to be built in the courtyard of Tengyeling and to remain there in retreat for the duration of his life. It was also made certain that future incarnations of this Rinpoche would be ineligible as candidates for the Regency.

Two nephews of Demo Rinpoche, Norbu Tsering and Palcho Losang, were given life imprisonment, along with many others, at Raggyap, a newly built prison. A monk named Nyagtrul and his tutor, Padma Tsering, were held directly responsible for placing the spell, as they were noted tantric practitioners who often worked with matters of the occult. Both these men were put in prison; Nyagtrul later committed suicide. It is believed that his anguished spirit caused many problems thereafter, leading to a subsequent exorcism which supposedly banished the spirit to dwell in a black *choten* down past Drepung Monastery. However, Nyagtrul was not to be so easily controlled, and the *choten* was soon found to have a crack on its side from which Nyagtrul was believed to have escaped. Since then, the spirit of Nyagtrul has been credited with numerous misdeeds.

One of the most serious outcomes of this incident was that all of the estates belonging to Tengyeling were confiscated by the government, save a few which had been acquired under special circumstances. This loss of property was a severe blow to the financial base of the monastery, and it led to a significant decrease in its power and status. Many of the residents of Tengyeling remained bitter against the government, and their relationship with His Holiness was also tarnished.

❀   ❀   ❀

In 1910 when the Chinese troops invaded Lhasa and His Holiness fled, leaving little rule behind him, Tengyeling saw the opportunity to improve its situation. Having a large food store and an internal well for drinking-water, it offered refuge to the Chinese, and it eventually became a Chinese stronghold. By 1911, the Chinese troops were well-established at Tengyeling, the monastery making a perfect fort with many of its inhabitants supporting the Chinese cause. It was especially difficult for my father and his men to approach the stronghold because there were no buildings nearby for taking cover. While fighting continued in other parts of the city, this stronghold held out, but the place was soon besieged by the Tibetans, who far outnumbered the Chinese. Periodically some shots were exchanged, and this continued until the Chinese ultimately surrendered.

Later, a fierce fight occurred near the Tsuglak Khang. A big block of buildings called Jiding Ling had several interlocking houses and passages. My father thought this was the point where he could break through to the southern part of the city. He picked his best men and, after an intense battle of two days, got into a

portion of the building the Chinese were holding. He then attacked through a passage, and his men made it into the adjacent
courtyard without losing many lives. Next there was only a third
courtyard and then the main gate, which faces a major road leading to the south, left to capture. Casualties on the Tibetan side
were much smaller than for the defending Chinese because
people living in the buildings were exclusively Tibetans. Moreover, they knew each and every one of the complicated network
of passages in the building. The Tibetans did not find much difficulty in securing the third and last courtyard and soon were
able to control the whole building. The difficulty then arose of
engaging the Chinese on the main road because they had ma-
chine-gun posts stationed on top of the surrounding houses. The
Chinese troops, in an effort to reenter the building, lost many
lives, and for several days things remained as they were.

During these encounters, one of my father's most gallant men,
Tsasha Tenpa, a tall Khampa, waited inside the gate and was
felling the Chinese with his sword when they tried to enter. They
were using fixed bayonets; the angle was such that they were
unable to shoot. The Chinese had thrown hand-grenades which
exploded inside and killed two men, but, strangely enough, nothing happened to Tenpa. The next time, he discovered a way to
protect himself, and each time the hand-grenades were thrown
in, he quickly took cover under a thick short wall built for un-
loading water buckets from the backs of carriers. Father told me
that that was Tenpa's lucky day, and through his bravery he had
disarmed and disabled at least six Chinese soldiers.

At dusk, one of the Chinese who was on my father's side
shouted out in Chinese that the Tibetans had fled, signaling that
they, the Chinese, were free to enter. When the troops came with
force into the courtyard, a burst of Tibetan fire came from all sides
and many were killed while others ran back outside. The Tibetans rushed out after them and were able to get to the other side of
the road and capture the house of Ragashar, which had been one
of the key positions of the Chinese for a long time.

Subsequent attacks on the southern part of the city soon
brought in building after building that the Chinese had used
as headquarters. Many of these buildings were the houses of

Tibetan nobles, including the houses of Samdrup Phodang, Tsarong, Shatra, Rampa, and Kunsangtse. When the Chinese occupied these buildings, the families of these great noble houses fled to various places; many of them took refuge in the big monasteries. Father was very helpful to the families when they returned to their homes, providing protection and food supplies, as there was a great shortage of these in Lhasa at that time.

Finally, the Chinese troops were no longer able to fight the Tibetans because they were not receiving any reinforcements and supplies due to the revolution in China. As soon as the news of the revolution reached Lhasa, a faction of the Chinese mutinied, thereby making the Tibetan forces even stronger than before. Father took advantage of this opportunity and through his influence on the ranks of the Chinese army, he was able to win a sizeable force over to his side. Foreseeing an inevitable defeat, the Chinese offered to surrender through the Nepalese representative in Lhasa. By this time, the Dalai Lama had reached Samding Monastery and was moving closer to the capital at Chokhor Yangtse Monastery, about forty miles from Lhasa. Father visited His Holiness often to report on the situation. His Holiness was now able to resume conducting all his state affairs. The Dalai Lama's Personal Representative, Tsatrul Rinpoche, who was in religious service at that time, arrived at the formal surrender with other senior officials. The formal surrender then took place witnessed by the representative of the Nepalese Government.

Now arose the question of deporting the Chinese troops. The Tibetan Government refused to permit them to go to China via eastern Tibet as they requested. Instead, they were permitted to leave only via India and only were allowed to carry some small arms for the security of the officers. Before their departure, Father gave a farewell dinner to the officers and there was much criticism of this action.

During the aftermath, Tibetan military officers made a thorough search of Yamon, the prior residence of the Chinese Amban (government representative) and a Chinese stronghold during the fighting for Tengyeling Monastery. Those Chinese found hiding were immediately deported, and many guilty monk conspirators disguised themselves in Chinese clothing and left with them. Because of such outright collaboration with the enemy, an official government enquiry was made. All land holdings were confiscated and Tengyeling was left as a skeleton. Demo Rinpoche was given enough provisions to survive, otherwise the guilty who were caught were sent to prison. Those not involved were sent home, and the remainder of the monks were distributed to other monasteries.

Many of the Chinese troops who sided with my father, and some others, were permitted to stay on. One Chinese officer named Th'an da ko married one of Father's nieces and later opened a restaurant next to our house called Chin Dai Zakhang, which means "Restaurant of the Commander General." It mainly catered to the twenty-five men of the bodyguard who were stationed at Tsarong House before proper barracks had been built at Norbu Lingka, the Summer Palace. Later, it was opened to the general public and became a successful business.

Another interesting person was known as Du Gen, a nickname used by Tibetans, which means "Elder Devil." Strangely, everybody knew him by this name. He was one of the volunteers who took part in pursuing His Holiness and his party when they escaped to India and who fought against Father at Chaksam. However, he became a friend after the war, and later, after I was born, he used to come to our house often to make kites for me. I remember my father used to say to him, "Tell my son stories about the war," but he just laughed and said nothing. He used to spend many hours with me making kites and painting them with beautiful designs.

Another man I remember was To Ma, who was also a kite maker and was well known in his profession. Other Chinese ex-soldiers who remained in the city engaged in work like embroidery and leather-tanning, or became restaurant owners, tailors, boot-makers, and so forth.

For the next few weeks preparations were carried out for the dispatching of the Chinese troops. Arms and ammunition were handed over to the government (via the Nepalese representative), and the government supplied transport and rations for their journey. In Lhasa there was great rejoicing to celebrate the peace, especially when the people heard that the Dalai Lama would soon arrive.

As the war came to an end, Father was the talk of the town, admired by all for his bravery and courage. Handsome and young, even the ladies admired him and were keen to be close to him. I learned from my aunt Tsering Dolma that at that time a very beautiful Lhasa girl was at his side as his mistress before his marriage was proposed to the House of Tsarong.

Towards the end of January 1912, the Dalai Lama, on his return to the capital, was received amidst great pomp and grandeur, and the procession proceeded to the Potala Palace. His Holiness arrived in Lhasa just before the Tibetan New Year and remained at the Potala for the next three months, during which time he was busy with important affairs of state and the usual religious ceremonies. One of the most important projects he undertook was to declare Tibet's independence. His Holiness was so engrossed in state affairs that he had overlooked making a clear announcement of his declaration of independence to the outside world. Perhaps he was lacking people in his service who had the knowledge of foreign languages to advise him on international rules and regulations, so his declaration was confined to Tibet only. In 1913, a conference was held at Simla between representatives of Tibet, China, and Great Britain. An agreement was initialed by the three parties but it was never ratified. Although China did not sign the treaty, Great Britain and Tibet did sign. The agreement included a map which demarcated the boundary between India and Tibet. At the same time Great Britain and Tibet signed a separate agreement on trade which cancelled the two previous treaties of 1893 and 1908 between Britain and China. Now Britain would trade directly with Tibet as an independent country.

4 Cabinet Minister and Commander-in-Chief

His Holiness gave appropriate titles and awards to all the men who served Tibet during his absence in India. My father was officially given the title of Dzasak (government official ranked directly under that of cabinet minister) and, together with his position as Chida (Commander General), he became known as *Chidza*. Meanwhile, the Dalai Lama had not forgotten the misfortunes that fell on the family of Tsarong. They were still suffering the loss of the head of the family, Tsarong Shapé Wangchuk Gyalpo, as well as his son, who had both been killed following accusations of being pro-Chinese. Tsawa Tritul, better known as Tsatrul Rinpoche, who was then an influential man in the Dalai Lama's service, proposed a marriage between my father and the widow of the late Tsarong Shapé's son. Tsatrul Rinpoche cleverly took the opportunity of arranging this marriage, as it so happened that the widow was Rinpoche's own sister. Rinpoche and his sister, Rigzin Choden, were from the Delek Rabten family, prominent Tibetans from Shigatse. Rinpoche's brother was married to Tsarong's daughter, Norbu Yudon, so the two families were already closely related.

The Dalai Lama immediately gave his consent to this marriage, wishing to help the Tsarong family, as well as my father, one of his favored assistants. At this time, Father had very little resources and His Holiness supplied him with the entire wardrobe, including formal robes, hats, boots, etc., that is required of a Dzasak. Government officials of all ranks wore very elaborate costumes at formal functions, which amounted to quite an expense. His

Holiness also gave him religious images, a rosary, horses, saddles, and two Tibetan seals bearing his title. He then sent Father off to the House of Tsarong with his blessing.

Although it had been agreed that Father would marry Rigzin Choden, the Tsarong's estate managers, head servants, and retainers gathered to express their concern about the continuation of the true descendants of the Tsarong family, which dated back many centuries. The result was a fresh proposition, unanimously agreed upon, that the widow Rigzin Choden would indeed be his first wife, while the eldest daughter of the late Tsarong Shapé, Pema Dolkar, should become the second wife to my father, in order to preserve the family lineage. A delegation of the servants supported by relatives put forward the proposal to the widow of the late Tsarong Shapé and the parties concerned, who, after a lengthy consideration, agreed without any objection.

Tsatrul Rinpoche was very pleased with this arrangement and always maintained a good relationship with my father; he often came to Tsarong House to discuss various matters. He was a great scholar, and when I came of age, I studied with him for almost two years. He also stayed in Japan and China for lengthy periods of time and knew much of the outside world. When the Chinese Communists came to Tibet, he was employed by the Chinese working for the *Tibetan Daily News* at Lhasa. His end came when a beggar pushed him to a fatal fall in one of the streets of Lhasa.

After two exiles and many years of experience and knowledge gained in other countries, the Dalai Lama was anxious to make Tibet a strong, independent country, and he took much interest in secular issues. He instructed Tsarong to organize an army using his knowledge of British and Russian military training that he had received during their exile in India and China. Tsarong's inclination was the same, and he gladly agreed to carry out the instruction and began to recruit the first fifty men of his modern army.

There were no army barracks built specifically for the troops, so he temporarily kept the men in Tsarong House, which had ample space to accommodate them. There was a large property beside old Tsarong House, and it was made a mess hall where all his men ate daily. Later it became the restaurant called Chin Dai Zakhang (Restaurant of the Commander General).

Father personally trained his small army of fifty men, twenty-five of whom were mounted guards for the Dalai Lama, accompanying His Holiness wherever he went. New army barracks were built near the Norbu Lingka, large enough to accommodate one thousand troops and officers. New recruitment and training had continued, and when the barracks were completed, he moved his men there.

Around this time, the Tibetan Government approached a Japanese ex-officer, Yasujiro Yajima, who happened to be in Lhasa, and asked him to train the newly recruited men in modern methods of warfare. Yajima agreed to do this and also helped to design the barracks at Norbu Lingka in the Japanese style, and he was given the responsibility of training a group of men in Japanese military methods. Another section was trained in the Russian system by Tenpai Gyaltsen, a Mongolian soldier, and a third in the British system of musketry. After his military instruction was no longer needed, Yajima stayed on for another five years before returning to Japan. His job was then to train the troops in physical drills and to give them swimming lessons. I was told by my father that Yajima was a peculiar man; he wished to be like the Tibetan officers and wanted to wear a headdress like theirs, with red ribbons in the knot. He was told that this red ribbon was an entitlement for the Tibetan officers only and therefore asked Father whether there would be an objection to his putting in a yellow ribbon instead of the red, and my father said this would be acceptable. Thereafter, he kept his hair long and began to tie it in a knot with a yellow ribbon.

The Government of Tibet had sent two young officers, Doring and Drumpa, accompanied by fifty soldiers from the Dalai Lama's bodyguard, to Gyantse for military training at British Military Headquarters. There were seventy-five Indian soldiers under two British officers at Gyantse who had been stationed there to protect the trade route. After their return to Lhasa, these two Tibetan officers became instructors to the newly recruited soldiers.

In accordance with His Holiness's desires, Tsarong continued to increase and organize the army. As the new battalions were being formed, they were numbered alphabetically, as *Ka*-1, *Kha*-1, *Gha*-1, etc., according to the Tibetan alphabet. Thus it was easy during future expansion of the regiments to simply add numbers once having completed the thirty letters of the alphabet. In this way, the army continued to increase its numbers to about ten thousand men by 1924. The first three regiments had one thousand troops in each, including the Dalai Lama's special bodyguard battalion; thereafter each regiment had five hundred men.

In 1914, it was decided by the government to send Kusho Mondhong Khyenrab Runsang to England for training in geology, along with three other young officers—Chang Ngopa Rinzin Dorje (Ringang), who studied electricity; Kyibuk Wangdu Norbu, telegraphy; and Gokhar Sonam Gonpo, military training. Mondhong was unable to use much of his knowledge in the field he was trained for, but he did serve His Holiness as his English interpreter for a brief period, and later joined the police force. Ringang was helpful in installing a small power station for the Norbu Lingka, and later the Tibetan Government built a power-house for supplying electricity to the whole city of Lhasa. His knowledge then became useful when the new mint was built at Drapshi. Ringang also served as His Holiness's main English interpreter. Because he stayed in England the longest of the four men, his English was the most perfected. Kyibuk worked at the telegraph office, but later became the English secretary to the Foreign Office of the Tibetan Government. Gokhar joined the bodyguard regiment, but unfortunately died shortly after.

The Government chose these four men from among its officials and invested in their training in England. Upon their return, they succeeded in making valuable contributions to Tibetan society. However, due to the general Tibetan dislike for anything new and innovative, they could by no means work to their full potential.

In 1915, after he was firmly established at Tsarong House, Father received a promotion and was given the title of Shapé (Cabinet Minister). He was also made Magchi Chewa, meaning "Supreme Commander-in-Chief" of the Tibetan army. These positions held great responsibility; among other things, Father was now fully in charge of the armed forces.

Towards the end of 1915, Tsarong informed His Holiness that a military parade could now be held for inspection of the troops. As decided by His Holiness, the parade was held in the spring of 1916. All through the winter, preparations were underway: new uniforms and Tibetan military flags, which had been designed and approved by His Holiness, were made. His Holiness had also given a detailed description of the Tibetan national flag, written in his own hand. Usually, official writing is carried out by the Chief Secretary, so when His Holiness the Dalai Lama writes something out personally, it is greatly treasured. This description was in the possession of my father until the year 1946, when it was given to the newly formed Foreign Office for preservation.

In the late spring of 1916, the great military parade was held near the Norbu Lingka, and demonstrations were given in the various military styles which had been taught. The whole city turned out to witness the display of troops and weapons, which the people had never seen before. It was at this time that His Holiness inspected the troops and selected the British musketry battalion as the group he preferred most. Thereafter, the whole army was trained in British musketry style.

Soon thereafter, Tsarong was awarded three medals by His Holiness. One gold medal (about three inches in diameter) was for his gallant work in organizing a modern army for Tibet. One silver medal was for attaining first place in the dismantling and assembling of Mauser pistols. The third medal was for coming in first in target shooting while on horseback. It was a very active and rewarding time in my father's life.

The military training and expansion of Tibet's army continued, but opposition both from nobility holding important positions in the government and from the monasteries grew gradually stronger. Rumors spread widely that the government planned to recruit soldiers from every district, and that taxes would be imposed on big landowners. Naturally the monasteries, as well as the noble families who were big landholders, would be the most seriously affected. The three great monasteries— Drepung, Sera, and Gaden—which were strongly represented in the National Assembly, also feared that their own power would be weakened by the rise of the military's power. Although His Holiness, inspired by his own knowledge of the outside world, encouraged him to pursue his endeavors, Tsarong had to face the growing opposition of the monastic community and a faction of conservative nobility. These groups hated innovation, army marching bands, the playing of football and polo—anything that was foreign or had to do with the West. They soon began to sow seeds of dissension between the Dalai Lama and the military. In spite of all these obstacles, a gradual increase in the army continued.

In addition to Father's post as the Commander-in-Chief of the Army, he also took on the duty of Mint Master, head of the Mint Department. The coinage of Tibet is somewhat complicated. Before 1900, the chief unit was the *trangka karpo*, a silver coin, which was cut into bits, and the pieces then used for smaller units. With the approval of His Holiness and the Government, Father set up a new mint at Norto Lingka, near the Norbu Lingka. The mint was called Sertam, meaning "gold coin," because it was mainly built for producing Tibet's first gold coin. In 1917, the first gold coin was minted, and its value was fixed at twenty *sang*. At that time the *sang* was the main unit of Tibetan money—one *sang* equaled roughly one Indian rupee. The *sang* was then broken down into smaller units; one *sang* equaled ten *sho*, one *sho* equaled ten *kar*, etc. Besides gold coins, copper coins had also been minted, and all the presses were powered by a giant water wheel. Copper was imported from India with great difficulty, but gold was more easily procured.

Each year the Government would put a large quantity of gold coins in the treasury at the Potala Palace as reserve. Tsarong foresaw that it was very important for the government to have a strong backing for the paper currency in circulation. Therefore, the gold coins were deposited in the government treasury at the Potala. In 1946, a certain amount of gold was imported from the United States when a Tibetan trade delegation visited that country. A large amount of gold in the reserve was taken out when the Thirteenth Dalai Lama's tomb was enshrined.

Besides the Sertam Mint, a separate department was established at Norto Lingka for weaving woolen material. Sorting out wool, carding, and dyeing was all done by hand. The material produced was a good quality tweed and my father once presented some to the Political Officer in Sikkim, Mr. F. Williamson.

While I was recovering from a dislocated elbow, we stayed at Gyantse where I got medical treatment from a British doctor who was stationed at the British fort there. At that time, Mr. Williamson was also staying at Gyantse, and he used to come visit us wearing a sport coat made out of this tweed material that he liked so much. Tsarong maintained a deep interest in the preservation and promotion of Tibetan handicrafts. During non-official hours, he could always be found wearing clothing made from this handwoven Tibetan woolen cloth; he did this though it was fashionable among others of his class and rank to wear the latest in fine brocades and silks imported from China. He put continuous effort into the weaving factory at Sertam, but when he left for India in 1924, it shut down from lack of interest. Later it was revived within the new Drapshi complex, but after a few years this factory too suffered the same fate, as it was then the fashion of the nobility, traders, and upper classes to wear imported woolens from India. Father, however, was always proud of the handwoven materials made by his own people and wore clothes made from these woolens throughout his life.

Between 1916 and 1918, Tsarong worked ceaselessly to strengthen the military in order to put down the Chinese menace in eastern Tibet. The Chinese had again occupied several districts in eastern Kham, and the Tibetan Government had sent strong reinforcements, but failed to expel them. More troops were rushed to the front with newly imported weapons, and eventually the Tibetans regained all of the many lost territories. These military successes were a direct result of the newly trained army at Lhasa and fresh supplies of arms and ammunition. Now over-confident, the Tibetan army was even planning to take over the border town of Tachienlu.

At this juncture, Chinese commanders at Ba, a province on the eastern border, approached Dr. Shelton, an American who was residing there as a Christian missionary. At the request of the Chinese authorities in Szechwan and Yunnan, the Government of China also approached the British Government for mediation between Tibet and China. The British Government sent Eric Teichman, who happened to be the Consulate General of the British Government stationed at Chengdu in Szechwan

Province. In 1918 the leaders gathered at Chamdo, and a temporary cease-fire was agreed upon. Both sides withdrew their forces
from the battle area; the new demarcation line was drawn at the
Drichu River. The eastern side of the river was the Chinese side,
and the western side would be under the Tibetan Government's
administration.

The border situation in the east was always uncertain, and
Tsarong was sure that peace could only be achieved through the
strength of the army. His wish was to make friendly contacts with
the neighboring countries and to gradually open up Tibet to the
outside world, breaking Tibet out of her long isolation.

❀   ❀   ❀

Pilgrimage to the Holy City of Lhasa is an important tradition in
Tibetan culture. There are actually a multitude of pilgrimage sites
throughout the country of Tibet, and Tibetan Buddhists will
travel long distances, sometimes enduring great hardships, to
make offerings at these holy places. Tsari is a very sacred and
famous pilgrimage center for Tibetans. It is near the Assam border, where the Tibetan Government has no administration; it is
a wild tribal land. In each Tibetan Year of the Monkey, which
occurs every twelve years, a large number of Tibetans undertake a pilgrimage tour there, headed by a government officer. It
is more of an adventurous trip than a peaceful pilgrimage. Opportunity arose for such a pilgrimage tour in 1919. The Dalai
Lama told Tsarong that he should accompany the pilgrims to
help them and at the same time to explore the area. He took
with him about 125 men from the bodyguard battalion for the
safety of the group; there were great dangers in the forest of Tsari,
as many people had previously lost their lives from treacherous
attacks by the tribesmen. The party left towards the end of December and soon reached Mikyim Ding, the gateway to the Tsari
sacred mountain. From Mikyim Ding one has to descend a trail
which leads round about mountainous terrain thickly covered
by forest. They camped in their tents and awaited the customary negotiation with the tribesmen to ensure a peaceful tour by
the pilgrims. A date had to be appointed for the tribal chiefs to

come to Mikyim Ding with their followers. At this negotiation meeting, the government representative tells them that the way should be cleared and that their people should be strictly ordered not to inflict any harm on the peaceful pilgrims during their holy walk. The government presents gifts to the tribal chief, including shells and beads, which they treasure greatly. On the negotiation day, a yak is tied up on flat land, and the tribesmen sit far away. If the negotiation is a success, they dash to the yak, pull it to pieces, and eat it there raw. The visitors watch anxiously while the yak is consumed in no time. Nothing is left on the field except the bones. This is a sign of their acceptance, and the visitors may then leave for the pilgrimage in safety.

The negotiation with the tribal chief was successful that year, and Father led the party onward. Beyond Mikyim Ding there is no road for horses and mules, and everybody must walk and carry their own luggage. The holy walk around this sacred mountain usually takes seven to ten days. The nights are spent without any shelter; sometimes people stop without even knowing their whereabouts for their night's sleep. At times the trail becomes so untraceable that they have to cut trees in order to clear the path. There are constant dangers from wild animals and snakes.

Accompanying Father was his mother, her second husband Lhundup La, his sisters Yungchen Dolkar and Tsering Dolma, and my uncle, Kalsang Lhawang. Pilgrims visiting the sanctuary were divided into four groups. When Tsarong, who led the first group, reached the first day's stop, there were no signs of the second group following him, so he had to send troops to see whether they were safely on their way. The next morning the first group had to remain where they were because the tribesmen had cut the bamboo bridge which was temporarily provided for the pilgrims. My father's party had to remain for three days before the bridge was repaired. Thereafter, the going was fairly smooth except for one night when the troops had to fire shots to frighten some tribesmen who tried to intrude into their camp. All groups returned to Mikyim Ding after a successful pilgrimage at Tsari. It is a very remote place, but one of the holiest pilgrimage sites in Tibet.

While the people dispersed from their groups and began the return journey to their respective homes, Tsarong left for Jayul and spent over a month planting tea as an experiment. During his stay there, a messenger came from home with news of my birth at Gyatso, where my mother was living. He soon left for home. Upon reaching Lhasa, he met His Holiness and reported his adventurous trip to Tsari and Jayul in detail, even showing photographs. We had many interesting pictures of these events, but unfortunately all of them were lost when they were left behind at Tsarong House in Lhasa.

Before I was born, my mother, Pema Dolkar, had given birth to two sons, but neither survived more than a few days. When my mother became pregnant with me, His Holiness advised her to move out of Lhasa to give birth to her child in order to save its life. So, with the permission of His Holiness, my father acquired Gyatso, a small house with a garden and farm land covering several acres, which belonged to the government. It was a very convenient place for my father because it was situated only about four hundred yards from Norbu Lingka where His Holiness's bodyguard regiment was stationed and where Father often had work.

My father was very pleased to see his newly born son, the heir to the Tsarong family, and immediately requested the Dalai Lama for the kind favor of granting a suitable name. His Holiness graciously granted this request and gave the name Dundul Namgyal, written in his own hand, and advised my parents not to take me to Tsarong House in Lhasa City. My mother was very protective and looked after me with great care at the house in Gyatso. Except for my mother, all other members of the family lived at Tsarong House in the city. However, they visited mother and the new baby at Gyatso frequently. Father was always shuttling between the two places, for he also had to attend the Kashag (cabinet ministers' office) in the city. He spent most of his time at Gyatso however, because after office hours, he was usually to be found at the Summer Palace with His Holiness, or at the mint or bodyguards' barracks, which were all near Gyatso. He always came home late when he was at the Palace—never earlier than eleven at night. Since most of his activities were centered around these three places, each had residential quarters for him.

One time while Father was at Gyatso, a sudden pain developed in his stomach. Soon after, my mother and my aunt, who happened to be staying at Gyatso, also had a similar pain. It was believed that they had received poison in their tea, and servants rushed to Lhasa to call for a doctor. Soon our family doctor, Shekar Amche La, arrived. After examining the tea, which was kept in the passage next to the room, he confirmed that aconite was present in it. Someone who had come to visit Father that morning had done the mischief. They were all completely cured however, and Father thought it wise to keep the matter hushed up.

When my father came into the Tsarong family, many debts had accrued from the running of the household. The family had undergone much hardship during the Chinese invasion in 1910-1912. With the execution of Shapé Tsarong and his son, they were left without men to look after the business of both the house in Lhasa and the Tsarong estate. They also suffered losses from being forced to abandon Tsarong House in Lhasa for many months during the Chinese occupation, leaving it open to pilferage and vandalism. After the war, around the same time that Father married into the family, he received Lhanga Estate, located near Shigatse, from the Government as a reward for the gallant defense of his country. Through the careful reorganization and management of both the Lhanga and Tsarong estates, he was able to slowly bring the family out of its financial difficulties. He also economized strictly in all the expenses of the household and sold many valuable objects, including the ornaments of the ladies, in order to clear the debts which had accumulated. He promised my mother that he would someday return all the jewelry which she had given up, and he was true to his word, eventually replacing it more lavishly than ever.

As the Tsarong family had many members of its own, he did not bring his own family into the house, but kept his mother, stepfather, and sister Tsering Dolma in a house opposite the old Tsarong House, called Tara Jhang. My father's sister Yungchen was married to Dingja Kusho, who had received artillery training at Quetta and later at Shillong in India. He became a general of the artillery brigade, although later he was removed from his post. He was a very humorous man and was liked by all. I regarded him as my elder brother, and we spent many years of happy times together.

My father's sister Tsering Dolma was married to Powo Kanam Depa. In the old days, marriages in Tibet were usually arranged by parents. Powo Kanam Depa was the chief of Powo District, which is close to the border with Assam. Kanam Depa was paying a nominal tax to the Tibetan Government, and he was more or less left to administer his district independently. During the Chinese trouble in Tibet between 1910 and 1912, he resisted the Chinese successfully, and thereafter, when the Dalai Lama came into full power, he refused to pay his taxes and did not allow government officials to enter his territories.

Tsarong's plan was that Tsering Dolma's marriage to Kanam Depa would bring about a settlement of the problem. He managed to invite Kanam Depa to Lhasa, and explained to him that it would be unrealistic and unsafe to remain in his old ways, advising him that his district should come under full control of the Government. He also said that if this proposal should come from him, Tsarong would recommend that the Government grant an appropriate title with estates for his livelihood. However, things did not materialize, and Depa left Lhasa with his party. Tsarong then sent a special messenger asking them to come back again. The chief would not come, but Tsering Dolma returned to Lhasa safely. Soon, the Government sent a strong force to deal with the people of the Powo district. The people put up a great resistance, but eventually the chief fled to the Indian border, where he died after an attack of dysentery. With the help of my father, Tsering Dolma managed to receive an estate as compensation from the Government. Though she later lost her estate, she was still alive when I left Tibet in 1957.

Soon my mother's younger sister, Tseten Dolkar, married Horkhang Dzasak. This old family had privilege of the use of the title *Dzasak*, which passed down to the heir of the family when he came of age. Her third sister, Norbu Yudon, married Delek Rabten, a nobleman from Shigatse, as was mentioned earlier. Tsarong Shapé Wangchuk Gyalpo's only living son, Kalsang Lhawang, was recognized as a reincarnate lama, and when he was young he was taken to Drepung Monastery for religious studies. He did not stay there, however, and was always coming back to the city. My father tried hard to help him in every possible way to start a career, but he did not succeed. Through Father's encouragement and force, my uncle joined the government service as a monk official and, later, as a police inspector in Lhasa. Sadly, fate led him to an addiction to alcohol, and he could not manage to take his job seriously. He died in middle age.

The two youngest daughters in the Tsarong family, Rinchen Dolma and Changchub Dolma, were eventually married to the two sons of Tsodrak Namgyal, the Crown Prince of Sikkim. The Prince escaped to Tibet in the year 1890, when the British forces entered Sikkim. The Government of Tibet gave the Prince asylum, along with the title of Rimshi and a large estate known as Taring. When the Prince refused to return to Sikkim to fulfill his role as Choegyal (king), his younger brother, Sidkeong Tulku, took the title. He ruled only a short time and passed away under mysterious circumstances. Afterwards, the third and youngest brother, Sir Tashi Namgyal, took reign as the Choegyal of Sikkim. The Raja of Taring remained in Tibet until his death in 1942.

By this time, Tsarong was a very powerful man in Tibet. His colleagues in the Cabinet feared him because he was very outspoken, yet they very much respected him as well. It is true he was hot-tempered, but he was also a man of great understanding. The expansion and training of the army continued under difficult circumstances. The question of raising taxes for maintaining the army arose. The Government proposed that large holdings of land, of both the nobles and monasteries, be taxed. The issue was discussed in the National Assembly, and taxing the estates of the Panchen Lama, who had been given extremely large estates during the rule of various Dalai Lamas, was suggested. It was decided that the Panchen Lama should contribute twenty-five percent and that the government would meet the balance for the defense of the country.

The decision to impose twenty-five percent of the defense expenditure on the Panchen Lama's estates was based on a complex history. During the period of the fourth Dalai Lama, the Khenpo (Abbot) of the Tashi Lhunpo Monastery at Shigatse, who was a brilliant scholar, became the tutor of the young Dalai Lama. The Khenpo was also an incarnate lama and his service to the Dalai Lama had been extremely good. To repay him, the Government of Tibet had given several estates to his monastery. As reward for his service, he was also given the title of Pandit, and later, the title of Pandita Chenpo, meaning "Great Pandit." After his death, being an incarnate lama, his reincarnation was found and called Panchen Lama. Henceforth, subsequent reincarnations were found and the title of Panchen Lama was established. Over a period of time, Tashi Lhunpo, the seat of the Panchen Lama, had accumulated several more estates. Tibetans often referred to Tashi Lhunpo as a second government due to its size. The National Assembly thus justified the imposition of this twenty-five percent tax. However, there existed bad blood due to misunderstandings between the Government and the Panchen Lama's office in Shigatse over the years, and this particular action caused further friction between the two, leading to the Panchen Lama's flight to China/Mongolia in 1923.

Regarding taxes, the National Assembly held a meeting to discuss the issue of additional taxes to be imposed on various holdings by the aristocratic families. A special reference was made to the *kalons* (ministers) and *depons* (army commanders). It was clear that the maintenance and training of the growing military regiments would require additional financial support from the Government. Although the meeting was about the defense of the country, not one representative was called from the Defense Department. Hence, a separate meeting was held at the army headquarters, and as a result, some officers went to the National Assembly meeting asking to see Kungo Ragashar outside. According to the standard government protocol, it would be highly inappropriate to approach the Assembly directly; therefore they requested to talk with a representative. Runi Ragashar was specifically requested because the officers had become well acquainted with him during his tenure as police officer. Unfortunately, he was absent on that day, and in his place Tsepon Lungshar came out to see them. He was a staunch opponent of the army and his handling of the situation reflected this. Perhaps argumentative exchanges took place between Lungshar and the military officers. What Lungshar reported to the National Assembly is not known; however, it created further unrest. Consequently, the Assembly began to panic based on a misinterpretation of the military's intention in approaching them like this. Apparently, the officers only went to question their lack of representation in a meeting called specifically to discuss military matters.

Unfortunately this action, together with the growing rumors of the military forces "plotting" to overthrow the government, caused a great deal of fear and panic. As a precaution, the Assembly called hundreds of monks to guard the Potala and Norbu Lingka Palaces. Guards were also placed at the residences of the Assembly leaders.

The Lonchen (Prime Minister), Sholkhang, then intervened and mediated between the two factions. He scolded the military leaders for causing such trouble during relatively peaceful times. From an investigation carried out by the Donyer Chenmo (Dalai Lama's chief secretary) further actions resulted. It is customary in Tibetan governmental procedure to declare both promotions and demotions at a *trungja*, the daily morning tea ceremony at the Norbu Lingka. This ceremony is orchestrated by the Donyer Chenmo, who is carrying out the direct orders of the Dalai Lama. The parties in question receive a notice, arrive at Norbu Lingka at nine o'clock in the morning, are served a cup of tea, and then the Donyer Chenmo declares his orders. In this case, officials from both the National Assembly and the Military were summoned to *trungja*. Shapé Kunsangtse, a conservative cabinet minister, was demoted along with Tsogo and Shankhawa, who were army officers. In addition, Lungshar and members of both factions were fined.

The military succeeded at getting one representative added to the National Assembly, as well as eliminating a staunch conservative from his post as Shapé. However, they suffered the loss of two of their most qualified leaders, and overall it could be said that this was the beginning of the downfall of military modernization. Rumors of a military coup circulated amongst the officials, and His Holiness began to question the wisdom of creating such a powerful force of arms.

Accomplishments in modernization, motivated by the shared vision of His Holiness, Tsarong, and others, reached their height in the early 1920s. With the help of two British telegraph engineers, Mr. King and Mr. Rosemeyer, telegraph lines were installed between Gyantse and Lhasa. Gyantse had already been linked with Gangtok, Sikkim since the Younghusband expedition. Kyibuk Wangdu Norbu, who had been trained in telegraphy in England, supervised the first telegraph office, which was in the Tengyeling compound. This opened up new possibilities for communication, as a message which previously took at least three days by horseback to reach Lhasa from Gyantse now took only minutes.

Another of the graduates from England, Ringang, single-handedly took on a plan to build a hydroelectric plant at Dode, a place about three miles from Lhasa behind Sera Monastery, where there was a small but forceful mountain stream. Machinery was ordered from England. The main power station at Dode was linked with a substation at Gyabumgang, providing all of Lhasa City with electricity for the first time.

Under the guidance of a British subject, Mr. Frank Ludlow, an English school was started at Gyantse. About thirty Tibetan boys, all sons of aristocrats, were selected to attend. It lasted only a few years and was then forced to close under pressure from the conservative faction.

More officers and men were sent to Gyantse for military training at the British military headquarters. Other officers were sent to Quetta and Shillong, India, where some were trained in infantry drills and others in artillery, cavalry, and gunnery. Another group was sent to Darjeeling to study for a military band. When the artillery group returned, they brought with them two ten-pounder mountain guns. Later, more cannons, machine guns, rifles, and ammunition were imported from India through arrangements with the British Government.

The country of Tibet is rich in natural resources, among them coal, oil, gold, silver, copper, crystal, mica, and iron ore. As mentioned earlier, these resources are not exploited, but there are some people who do privately dig for gold on their land and sell it in the market. These dealings are secretly handled because should it be known that gold was dug from one's land and sold, one would be taxed by the State.

There was a period when Father wanted to open up the country for its rich deposits. Sir Henry Hayden was invited to Tibet from India in 1922, and geological surveys were conducted in the northern and southern parts of Tibet. Kusho Mondhong accompanied him during the tour, and as a result of their visit, some mica, iron ore, and coal samples were brought to Lhasa. Later, with persisting superstitions and omens in the minds of the people, criticism and adverse rumors developed. Because of this strong resistance, the Dalai Lama hesitated to pursue this matter, and thereafter Father had to discontinue his mining explorations.

The uneasy feelings continued amongst the leaders of the monasteries, who were supported by a large section of conservative lay and monk officials of the government in their reaction against the buildup of the army. Moreover, they believed that bringing in foreigners who helped with linking telegraph lines with the outside world, setting up English schools, constructing better roads, and excavating mines, as well as sending officials to train outside Tibet who brought back new innovations, would all seriously influence the minds of people who were dedicated to their religious life. They believed that excavating the earth and taking precious minerals was sacrilege; that the areas bearing these precious materials were guarded by deities who would be offended by these acts. It would be unfair to criticize these monastic leaders too much, because it was their cherished faith in Buddhism and their desire to protect their religion that brought them to these positions. Such feelings existed in those times because of the isolated nature of the country and its inhabitants. On the other hand, the Dalai Lama, who had seen and gained much knowledge of the outside world, seriously wanted to benefit his people by supporting the gradual development of Tibet.

Towards the end of 1923, events led to a strong action by the Dalai Lama against the Loseling College of Drepung Monastery. A close collaboration with the Chinese by some members of this college was revealed from old documents confiscated from Tengyeling Monastery during the 1910-1912 invasion. It was common knowledge that when the Government requested monks from Drepung to assist in the defense of Lhasa, they refused. In addition, officials from the Loseling College itself protected the Chinese Amban during the uprising in 1911. So it was easy to understand why there was much tension between Loseling and the Tibetan Government for so many years. In 1920, an arrest of three managers of the largest Houses in Loseling College was carried out by Ara Karpo, the Donyer Chenmo. The charges against them concerned some matter of estate ownership; however, there must have been other motivations as well. One of these managers was released soon after, but the other two remained in prison in the Shol enclave. The monks of Loseling were infuriated by these arrests and held a demonstration; over one thousand gathered together and proceeded en masse to Norbu Lingka. They went to prostrate before His Holiness and make an appeal for the release of the prisoners. Some of the younger monks however, made rather unpleasant scenes in the Palace compound, causing much confusion and some damage. Upon receiving an urgent telephone call at the Kashag, the ministers rushed to the Palace and tried to calm the monks. By evening they had managed to persuade the monks to return to their college, which was about three miles from the Palace.

Tsarong was ordered by His Holiness to take strong measures to deal with the monks of Loseling, but he was firmly instructed that bloodshed must be avoided at all costs. The Kashag met, and Father proposed to use his military might, but this was not favored by his colleagues. In spite of the lack of support for this action by the government, Father left for the bodyguard headquarters and issued instructions to move a strong force of about two thousand armed men to the area of Norto Lingka and set up a temporary command post at Kyitsel Luding. Norto Lingka was about a mile away from Drepung, yet the troops were strategically placed to block the road from Drepung to the Norbu Lingka Palace where His Holiness resided. It was a non-threatening but firmly defensive move made by my father. He also deployed all the men in His Holiness's bodyguard to protect the Palace. He then sent a special messenger to the heads of Loseling

College informing them that he would personally come to Dhampak, a village below the monastery, with only a civilian staff, to discuss a peaceful settlement of the issue. Early the next morning, all troops were in position with their commanding officers, and Tsarong, after having a brief conversation with the officers on his way, headed straight for the village. Representatives from Drepung arrived, and together with Tsarong, they discussed a settlement of their grievances. Father explained to them that the incident at the Palace had hurt His Holiness's feelings and that he had been disheartened to see such behavior as this by lamas in their religious robes. He assured them that if the men who organized the demonstration were handed over to him, he would personally see that the lives of the demonstrators and those who were responsible would not be endangered. Furthermore, he stated that if this was done, he would guarantee that the punishment of the men would be as lenient as possible. Father practically begged them, using "we," as in, "we must find a peaceful solution," so as to emphasize the common ground they had in their respect for their spiritual leader, the Dalai Lama. However, no decision could be made on the spot because the representatives had to go back to Drepung for discussion with the other leaders. Father then returned to Kyitsel Luding for the night.

The next day, Tsarong again met the representatives, and the men who organized the demonstration were handed over to him. Around sixty monks were arrested. They were imprisoned for a period and they received a light punishment for their grave deeds. They then were turned over to some noble families who were to look after them, keeping them under something like house-arrest. The prisoners had iron bars on their legs, yet because they were lamas, their treatment was lenient. Years later, many of these monks became members of the households; some served in the private family chapels as keepers and others even became stewards.

His Holiness was pleased that the matter was successfully resolved without violence or bloodshed. The relationship was now more or less cleared between the Dalai Lama and the unruly factions at Loseling College. However, tension mounted between the military (and therefore my father) and the conservative monastic community. This tension would only increase in the years to come.

5 Tibet's Modern Army

While the expansion and modernization of the army continued
full speed, the Dalai Lama thought that it was necessary to organize and update the city police force of Lhasa in accordance with
modern methods. So, the Government of Tibet invited Sardar
Laden La, who was then the Superintendent of Police at
Darjeeling. On loan from the British Government, Laden La arrived and introduced modern training. A police force of three
hundred men was recruited, and many Tibetan Muslims joined
the service. They even had their own marching band with bag-
pipes and bugles, as some band instructors from Darjeeling were
called in to instruct this special police band. Working together
with Laden La was Kur Mondhong, who officially headed the
police department along with Phuntsok Rabgye Ragashar.
Ragashar later became Commander-in-Chief of the army, as well
as a Shapé.

The Dalai Lama greatly appreciated Laden La's service, and
conferred on him the title of Dzasak. A few Tibetans may have
been jealous of this title as Laden La was not a Tibetan subject,
yet he attained this high rank of the government in a relatively
short period of time. Laden La remained in Lhasa for over a year;
his service was not confined to police organization alone, but included giving suggestions on military expansion. The police force
itself was well organized; having its own marching band and
smart uniforms made it the envy of others. This caused much
rivalry between the police and the army, and the friction between
the two groups led to a particular incident in May 1924. It happened that one day some troops from the *Gha*-l regiment an-
tagonized some policemen, resulting in a fight. Upon learning

the news, Tsarong, along with Sardar Laden La, officers and other men, rushed to the scene. They managed to stop the fight in time, before some of the soldiers who had gone to the barracks to collect arms had returned. There were many stabbings, and the guards arrested all of those at the scene. A lengthy interrogation then began, and all participants were questioned by the officials.

Years later, my father was to give me an old-style Tibetan scroll, consisting of more than five hundred lines of Tibetan script that detailed the events and the enquiry which followed. At that time it was customary during interrogations to take extensive notes for the police records and the investigating committee's report. Unfortunately, this valuable historical document was left behind in Lhasa.

As a result of the enquiry, Tsarong, with the support of some other officials, passed judgment on the guilty parties. The punishment was the cutting off of one man's leg and the same for a second offender's ear. Unfortunately, the man whose leg was severed passed away not long after. These punishments may appear extreme, but they were common throughout Tibet's history. However, His Holiness had previously made a ruling to outlaw capital punishment as well as amputations, and so Tsarong's judgment caused a good deal of controversy. The antimilitary factions used this incident as fuel for their argument that the military, led by my father, was becoming too powerful to control, and that His Holiness's authority was threatened.

Rumors persisted that Tsarong's arrogance and strength were growing too great and there was talk of a military coup. His Holiness began to experience great pressure from his more conservative cabinet ministers and monk officials. Regarding his harsh decision, Tsarong thought it was important to have firm control over the military and police forces and insisted that it was necessary to take serious action at that time in order to prevent further trouble. He remained steadfast in this belief, and despite the rumors, kept a close relationship with His Holiness. He was with the Dalai Lama at least every other day, whether or not there was any work to be done. Despite all of the controversy during that time, this relationship was a fact that could not be disputed.

Sometime after this clash between the army and police, Sardar Laden La left the service of the Tibetan Government and returned to his family in Darjeeling. Others also felt it was time to go, but were not as fortunate in their departure. A certain Major Padma Chandra, who was better known as Pema Tsendra, came from India as a drill instructor and served under Tsarong. As the environment became more tense, he must have felt he was in danger and fled through the South, thinking it the shortest route back to India. Unfortunately he was pursued by troops who caught up with him on the Gokhar Pass, two days' journey from Lhasa. Apparently he must have resisted because there on the Pass he was shot and killed.

I have a distinct memory of soldiers visiting our house out in Gyatso. I, a young boy of four and a half years, was sitting outside on my nanny's lap, and four or five soldiers were exchanging violent stories, perhaps somehow intending to frighten or tease me. One man pointed to another tall soldier, whose name was Major Kalsang, and claimed that it was he who shot Pema Tsendra on the Pass. They also told a horrible story about the Chief Secretary, Donyer Chenmo, whose nickname was Ara Karpo, meaning "white bearded." He was the main representative of the conservative monastic party, which was against all and any innovations, including the modernized armed forces. The soldiers told me that Ara Karpo had been decapitated and at that moment his head was being fried in a pan, his captors using their bayonets to stir it about. This, of course, was not true, but it gives a good indication of the mood at that time between the army and the establishment.

With the help of Sardar Laden La, Mondhong and Ragashar had developed the Lhasa police, which was well on its way to becoming a modernized force. It was thoroughly trained, and discipline and order within the city soon improved under its charge. However, there was one month out of every year when their power was rendered useless, and that was the first month of the year in the Tibetan calendar, usually falling somewhere around February or March.

According to Tibetan tradition, His Holiness the Dalai Lama made a ruling that during this month, all authority of the city magistrate was transferred to the Shalngo, administrative monks from Drepung Monastery. The Shalngo acted as the city magistrates during this month, as well as for nine days during Tsongcho, a smaller prayer festival which falls in the second month. There were two leaders of these Shalngo working with twenty-one Geyog (special enforcers), and assisted by roughly fifty Thabyok. The Thabyok were actually lay people from Dhamba village, just below Drepung Monastery. They were officially enlisted as kitchen helpers for the nearly twenty thousand monks who participated in the prayer assembly; however, they also assisted the Shalngo when possible. It was these relatively few monks and lay people who were responsible for protecting and directing the over one hundred thousand people who flooded into the city during the Losar (New Year) and Monlam Chenmo (Great Prayer Offering Festival) celebrations.

Losar, the Tibetan New Year, actually takes place over three days and is one of the most important celebrations of the year. Thousands come from all over Tibet on pilgrimage to the Holy City to make prayers and offerings before the image of Jowo Rinpoche in the Tsuglak Khang. During this month, the population increases dramatically, but most of the people are orderly and well-mannered, and usually there are not too many problems.

Another important celebration, Monlam Chenmo, the Great Prayer Offering Festival, begins on the second day of Losar and continues through to the twenty-eighth day of the first month. During Monlam Chenmo, on the fifteenth day of the first Tibetan month, falls Chenga Chopa, when magnificent prayer offerings are made in the street around the Tsuglak Khang. These offerings, called *chopa*, are fashioned of butter, intricately worked, beautifully colored, and then placed along the Barkor with butter lamps, which glitter in the night. The fifteenth day of the Tibetan month always falls on the full moon, and it is a unique pleasure to watch these offerings in the moonlight. Each offering is twenty-five to sixty feet high, and in between three or four of the best *chopa*, elaborate stages are erected where people perform puppet shows. The Dalai Lama attends this annual ceremony with all his ministers and government officials. During the prayers, he inspects the offerings and makes careful notes, later giving prizes to the most beautiful ones. Before the Dalai Lama proceeds in his grand procession around the city, the body-guard and other battalions are posted throughout the Barkor (middle circle-street around which the *chopa* are displayed), and a band playing fifes is assembled to accompany the procession. All incoming streets are cordoned off by ropes, and the crowd is held back by Simchungpa—lay troops from the old-style army in full ancient regalia. The Simchungpa remain in place until the Dalai Lama safely returns to the Tsuglak Khang. When the cordon is lifted, the crowd bursts out like a river and passes through the Barkor to have a glance at the wonderful offerings. Later in the night, groups of dancers from various country districts wander around merrily and dance till well past midnight.

In 1923, construction began on the new Tsarong House, which was built on a flat piece of land measuring about fifteen acres, chosen for its beautiful and tranquil view. Unlike the houses of other nobles, it was built on the outskirts of Lhasa City near the Kyichu River. From this site, which was thickly covered with trees, one had a beautiful view of the surrounding peaks enclosing the city. To the northwest, the majestic Potala Palace, with its gleaming golden roofs, stood upon its own hill. Towards the north, one could see the Holy City, and in the southeast was the Bumpa Ri, a mountain whose tallest ridge is shaped like a vase. The Kyichu River flowed in front, not very far from the house, although one couldn't see it from the house due to the dense forest.

The house itself was a two-storied, rectangular building containing thirty-six rooms of different sizes. Concrete steps in front of the house led to a big hall. The hall had beautiful carvings on the wooden beams and pillars, and exquisite drawings and paintings on the walls. Doors from this hall led to the eastern and western suites, and an inner door led to a staircase going up to the second floor of the mansion. This main hall was large and spacious, measuring thirty feet by thirty feet, and in later years my older children used to skate in it when they came back for their winter vacations, using roller skates brought from India. Four large store rooms lay behind the main suites and hall on the ground floor. The upper floor contained a similar hall, which was set aside as the main family chapel, known to everyone in the house as the Choegyal Khang. This name, meaning "The House of the Religious Kings," was given because images of three religious kings of Tibet were enshrined there.

On the direct advice of the Dalai Lama, life-size images of the three celebrated kings of Tibet, Songtsen Gampo, Trisong Detsen, and Ngadhak Trirel, were enshrined as symbols of our humble faith in their great works. These images were made out of copper and gilded. Costumes were made of the highest quality brocade, completed with ornaments with solid gold settings and precious jewels. Amber beads placed around the necks of the images had been imported from Germany. They were seated in frames with exquisite wood carvings and a glass front. Daily offerings were made before them. The most important part of this display was that inside the images were *sung shuk*, numerous objects that are considered highly sacred. These objects included relics, printed prayers and mantras, small pieces of robes and hairs of famous lamas, medicines, and pills made by celebrated lamas and physicians, precious stones, and many other valuable objects which were inserted when the images were initially consecrated by high lamas. Among these *sung shuk*, the most important were the relics of the Lord Buddha, given to my father at Benares by His Holiness the Thirteenth Dalai Lama. This was by far the most sacred room of the house. It was a sad moment when I was told that during the Chinese Cultural Revolution in the late 1960s, Red Guards entered our house and the three life-size images were thrown out of the window and smashed. Nobody knows what happened to the precious ornaments with which they were adorned.

The walls of the Choegyal Khang were lined with scriptures and *thangkas* (religious paintings), and a large altar in the center of the room was full of offerings, butter lamps, and incense which burned continuously throughout the day and night. All family ceremonies and prayer gatherings took place in this room. A corridor from the staircase led to the east and west wings. Each suite contained a spacious living room, a bedroom, a private prayer room, a bathroom, a large storeroom, and an office. One of the living rooms set aside for our guests was pillarless, and iron beams were substituted for wooden ones, which was much of a novelty to our relatives and friends at that time.

A library containing many foreign books, a guest suite, and a banquet hall were situated behind the family rooms. Besides passages and servants' quarters, there was another room very important to the family. This room contained the shrine of the family deity, the Goddess Palden Lhamo, and a resident monk was specially charged with looking after this room, making offerings to Palden Lhamo on behalf of the members of the Tsarong family.

The house was, on the whole, well planned and spacious, including modern windows with glass panes, which were much talked about in Lhasa, as houses in Tibet did not have glass windows at that time. Behind the main mansion, a long line of one-storied houses stretched from west to east, leaving the front open for a garden. The western side of these outer houses contained two kitchens, a guest house, and storage rooms for fuel. Behind, in back, were four servants' quarters and the lavatories. The chain of buildings on the east side contained the stables and the cow shed as well as a guest house where our Austrian friends, Heinrich Harrer and Peter Aufschnaiter, later lived. In addition to the front garden, there was a fruit and vegetable garden on the west side and a huge park in the back of the house, which ran wild with trees like a miniature forest.

The plans of this house were drawn up by my father with ideas formed from his visits to India, China, Russia, and Outer Mongolia. He brought back many modern ways to the traditional life of Tibet. The house became sensational news and most talked about because of its modern appearance. It took a year and a half of hard work to complete. As Father was then very busy with his work in the Government, he put his younger brother Phuntsok Norbu to supervise according to plans and to see to its progress. However, Father often visited the construction site himself to oversee the work. Many years later, Tibetans took to building their houses in this modern fashion because, being out of the city, it was cleaner and more comfortable in the midst of trees and nature.

In 1924, a big military display was organized at Drapshi Field. Troops were called from other stations and some five thousand men assembled. The show lasted three days, and all the ministers and government officials attended the function. Thousands of people, both lay and monastic, came to watch the parade. It was their first time seeing the modern guns being fired in large numbers. There were six ten-pounders in the artillery regiment; these greatly impressed the public. I was then very young and was taken to the show from my home at Gyatso. I still clearly remember the incident. When I heard the guns booming in the distance, even before reaching Drapshi, I cried and refused to go any further. My mother, who was accompanying me with the servants and escorts, had to send me back to Gyatso!

Despite the success of the increasing modernization of the armed forces, opposition to Tsarong was present and growing. Many officials did support him, but one cabinet minister, along with the conservative heads of the monasteries and noble families, continued to object to his actions and powerful status. In response to these objections, Father repeatedly submitted the resignation of his three posts as Cabinet Minister, Commander-in-Chief of the army, and Mint Master. According to Charles Bell, who was a good friend of Tsarong at that time, his resignation stated that:

> I am a man of the common people; I am not a member of the aristocracy. I am man without learning. Thus, I am unable to render good service. I therefore beg to be relieved of my three posts. If not of all three, then of two. If not even of two, then at any rate of one.*

Tsarong offered these resignations directly to His Holiness the Thirteenth Dalai Lama, who then referred them to the Kashag as was the custom. None were ever accepted.

In September 1924, Tsarong told His Holiness that he wished to take leave to go on pilgrimage to India and suggested that on his way he could inspect the mint at Norbu Tsokyil in Dromo. He also offered to discuss with the British Government further military training in India. The Dalai Lama agreed to his requests and granted a leave of absence. It was at this time that the tension reached a high point with the conservative factions in

---

* (From *Portrait of the Dalai Lama* by Charles Bell, (London: Collins Press, 1946), p. 301.

opposition to the military and police officials. Plots and intrigues abounded, rumors were thick that Father and other powerful officers were planning to overthrow the government.

The day Tsarong left for India, he visited the Dalai Lama at the Palace to take his leave. They discussed governmental matters and this delayed our departure. My mother told me that we all left the house together, but my father went to the Palace while we waited at a place called Kyitsel Luding, about a mile away from the Norbu Lingka. I was just under five years old when I was taken to India with my parents for the first time. Since I had always been kept at Gyatso, I had never seen Lhasa; I was first to visit Calcutta. We waited for my father to come. Our party consisted of my father and mother, myself, a nanny, our cook, and a few servants. My sister Kunsang Lhakyi, who was just born the year before, was too young to travel and was left behind in Gyatso. Father was much delayed at the Palace, and we could only go about five miles that day. We also had to stay an extra day or two along the way at the request of relatives and friends. We then arrived at Dromo where the mint had been established for producing copper coins. My father stayed there for about two weeks, and, as I was so young at the time, I can only remember seeing some machines. When I was taken out by my nanny, I recall seeing a giant water wheel which was a great amusement to me; I used to visit it every day.

Eventually our family left for India, crossing the Jelep La Pass, and finally reached Gangtok, Sikkim. There, Father was greeted by Chang Ngopa (Ringang), who was returning from his second period of study in England. Chang Ngopa was riding an imported motorcycle that he intended to bring back to Lhasa, despite knowing full well the current attitudes towards new innovations, which included motorized vehicles. Upon arrival in Lhasa, Chang Ngopa presented this motorcycle to His Holiness as a gift. It was clear he would not be permitted to use it, given the political climate of that time.

We then proceeded on to Kalimpong in West Bengal. Before leaving for Calcutta, my father spent several days in Kalimpong, where many old friends came to meet him. Among these were Raja and Rani Dorji of Bhutan House, Mr. David Macdonald, who had helped my father when he was fleeing to India in 1909, and many others. Rinchen Dolma, one of my mother's younger sisters, joined our party there in Kalimpong. She was on winter leave from school in Darjeeling where she had been studying for several years. Rinchen Dolma was of great assistance on our travels, as her English was good and she could help with the interpreting. She was quite responsible and mature for her fourteen years. We also spent one week in Darjeeling, visiting the Laden La family. Later they joined us in Calcutta, as did several friends and relatives who were passing through the city.

The British India Government appointed Rai Bahadu Norbu Dhondrup as our official guide and interpreter, and he accompanied Father during his entire visit through India and Nepal. Upon reaching Calcutta, the Government gave us a good reception; we initially stayed at the Grand Hotel, which was a fine establishment. However, as there was a great deal of shopping and subsequent repacking of goods for shipment back to Lhasa, we later shifted to a private residence where there was more room to work.

During this time, Tsarong purchased an automobile, a brown Dodge convertible, which was used often during local pilgrimages and shopping excursions. I am sure he intended to take it back to Lhasa, but as news reached us of the strengthening resistance of government officials towards "new innovations," he must have changed his mind and sold it before our departure. Although we were far removed from our home, there were always travelers coming and going, bearing news and letters which kept Father abreast of the political situation.

In Calcutta, Father went to inspect Fort William and other places of interest, including the Calcutta Museum and Zoological Garden. One day he was taken to Dum Dum Airport, which was then a restricted military airport prohibited to the public, and watched the planes flying. He was asked if he wanted to fly in a plane to see Calcutta from the air, but he declined the offer. Another day, we were taken to Calcutta Port to see the ships. A number of battleships happened to be in Calcutta at that time, and we visited one of these. The ship was taken out to sea and he saw the guns being fired. My father was asked to fire a gun and he did so. I remember the Captain gave me a toy, a lion made out of papier maché, and its head moved when pushed. I kept this toy for many years after.

After spending several days in Calcutta seeing all the Buddhist centers, we left on pilgrimage to Nepal. The King of Nepal sent his officials to receive our party at Raxaul, the last railway station on India's side of the border. All transport arrangements were made by the Nepalese Government. Tsarong had an excellent relationship with the Nepalese Legation in Lhasa. In fact, the King and my father became close friends, and his son and I were to become friends as well. While His Holiness the Fourteenth Dalai Lama was attending the 2,500th anniversary of Lord Buddha in 1956, some of the officials accompanying him told me that a certain Nepalese army major, Mahindra, was inquiring after my whereabouts. I thought this was the son of the Nepalese Legation at Lhasa, my old friend. I made inquiries about this gentleman through my Nepalese friends, but to no avail. Besides, my father had known many Nepalese traders who were settled in Lhasa, and had many close connections with them. However, it was these affiliations which would eventually work against his reputation.

From Raxaul onwards, there were no proper motorable roads. We drove our cars as far as we could and then had to cross the pass into Nepal. The government had arranged dandies, that is, covered chairs supported by poles which were carried on men's shoulders. Along the way, Father learned that the King of Nepal was nearby on a hunting trip. He arranged for a meeting to pay his respects. In return, the King sent his son with presents to our camp.

After crossing the pass, we came to the capital, Kathmandu, where Tsarong was received by high-ranking military officers, and a formal reception was staged in tents. He was honored with a salute of guns, and a guard of honor was provided. He was then taken to the Palace in a traditional chariot.

We stayed in Nepal for about two weeks, and during this time the Government of Nepal arranged a display of military drills and of guns in action. Father was also taken to see the armory. Thereafter, he visited the temples and sacred shrines. During his stay, many Nepalese traders came to meet him, discussing trade between Nepal and Tibet. Before our departure, the Nepalese Commander-in-Chief gave a farewell banquet.

We returned by the same way we had come and proceeded to Calcutta. Father then went to Bombay for a brief visit, while mother and I waited behind. The visit to India and Nepal went successfully; when the news reached Lhasa, it became quite a sensation. During Tsarong's long absence from home, the various groups from the monasteries and conservatives amongst the government officials had time to prejudice His Holiness against him. They perpetuated many rumors and used them to pressure His Holiness into taking action. All sorts of stories had been fabricated, especially by one man, Lungshar, who was another favorite of the Dalai Lama, but a rival to Tsarong. He and the Donyer Chenmo shared a deadly hatred for the army. Even the Dalai Lama's nephew, Drumpa Dzasak, who was second to the Commander-in-Chief, went to the Dalai Lama with tears in his eyes to influence him against the military. Many fantastic stories were circulating among the government ranks, one of which involved a certain monk official named Khenchung, who was the Tibetan Trade Agent in Gyantse. He claimed to have had a private audience with the Dalai Lama in which His Holiness stated that he possessed a document, written and signed by Tsarong and other military officials, that outlined their intention to take all temporal power away from His Holiness. Khenchung repeated this story to the Political Officer of Sikkim, Mr. F. Williamson, who then reported it to the Foreign Secretary of the British India Government, as was standard procedure with information such as this. These documents are now available to the public. In Williamson's report, he relays Khenchung's story, along with a considerable amount of doubt. He was particularly skeptical because Khenchung claimed never actually to have seen the document referred to by His Holiness, and because Khenchung waited over a year to report this information and even then did not approach him directly.

During Tsarong's absence from Lhasa, His Holiness, under the influence of the conservative officials, began taking action against the military. All experienced commanders and several trained officers were demoted, and in their place government officials who had no experience of any kind in military affairs were posted. As the army commanders were removed, they were charged with minor offences against the State, such as not resuming the traditional long hairstyle after returning from military training in India, or other simple charges. When the bodyguard general, Depon Surkhang, was discharged, he was accused of leaving his house and living separately with his mistress. In this way many of the officials who shared the vision of progress towards a modernized Tibet were eliminated, and the conservative faction gained the power that they had so long struggled to obtain.

Tsarong then began his return trip to Lhasa, spending a few days more at the mint at Dromo. The Tibetan Government was now well linked by telephone, and they were getting detailed information about where my father was and when he would be arriving. Two days' journey from Lhasa, at a halting place at Chushul, he received a message, by special courier, conveying orders from the Government informing him that his service as Commander-in-Chief of the army was no longer needed. The country was at peace and there was nothing much to do in the Defense Office. He was ordered to continue to attend the Kashag as usual. As previously mentioned, all official declarations of demotions, etc., were carried out by the Donyer Chenmo during the *trungja* ceremony. No one had ever received such an order via courier, so it was clear that His Holiness did not regard this as a typical demotion.

Much later, in 1940, when my father was accompanying my mother to Calcutta for medical treatment, his friend Kunphel La related all the intrigues played out against him during his absence in 1924-1925. Kunphel La met my father on several occasions in both Kalimpong and Calcutta. During one of the meetings, at which I happened to be present, he confirmed many of the things my father had heard earlier. The oddest story he told was that Drumpa Dzasak had informed the Dalai Lama that the military was to overthrow the Government, and that Tsarong had even received a salary from the Nepalese Government to fund this undertaking. Father was shocked to hear these stories. Why would he contrive such plots and then immediately leave for India? And why would he return to Lhasa if he had been guilty and running away? Moreover, everything made little sense given the close relationship Tsarong had with His Holiness.

After his return, Father went to see His Holiness to pay his respects and offer some things which he had brought from India. He had purchased several grand presents especially for the Dalai Lama, including brightly colored parrots, goldfish, and a tall, fine, porcelain vase made in China. Many people were surprised to see Tsarong arrive at the Palace in such a gracious manner; perhaps they expected Father to be bitter about the termination of his post, but this was not the case. His Holiness received him in equal graciousness, and although Father came in the morning, the visit did not end until late in the evening.

During their conversation, it was said that my father, in regards to his dismissal, had asked His Holiness, "How strange. What did I do [wrong]?" His Holiness did not seem to have taken notice of the question, and changed the subject to other matters. This account was told to me by friends, but Father never mentioned anything about it. Since he had been intimately close with the Dalai Lama, such a question could have been asked, otherwise it was a breach of the strictest protocol to put such question directly to him. Tsarong continued to attend the Kashag daily, but his relationship with the Dalai Lama was not quite the same as before. With the continuous criticism against him, the Dalai Lama removed Tsarong from the post of Cabinet Minister in 1929. Under the supervision of inexperienced commanders and officers, both the army and police forces were allowed to deteriorate from their high standard of the early 1920s.

❀   ❀   ❀

The 1920s was a period of great political challenge for Tsarong; it was also a very active time in his personal life. His first wife, Rigdzin Choden, had no children, and although she remained in Tsarong House for many years, when I was eight years old she left our house and became a nun. Rigdzin Choden was always a deeply religious woman; she was also a caring aunt, loved by all the children. Tsarong had two children by my mother, Pema

1. D. D. Tsarong. Originally captioned, in German, "The General with the *Dutt* [topknot], the High General of the Tibetan Army, Tsarong Shapé."

5. His Holiness the Fourteenth Dalai Lama, Tenzin Gyatso.

6. His Holiness the Thirteenth Dalai Lama arriving at Peking railway station, 1908.

7. Another view of His Holiness' arrival at Peking railway station, 1908.

8. Preparations for His Holiness the Thirteenth Dalai Lama's departure for Tibet from Kalimpong, India, 1912.

9. General Tethong Gyurmey Gyatso (center front) resting his foot on the mountain gun which was captured at the battle of Jyekundo after defeating the Chinese, 1916.

10. D. D. Tsarong with Mr. David Macdonald, who helped Tsarong during his escape to India in 1910. Kalimpong, India, 1940.

11. Chaksam Monastery at the Chaksam Ferry, where D. D. Tsarong engaged in a strong rear-guard action, holding back the Chinese pursuers in 1910. This picture shows the Tibetan side of the position.

12. Left to right, standing: Depon Salungpa, unknown, Sampho Palden Choewang, T. Tsering, Depon Dingja Dorji Gyaltsen, Penpa Tsering, Phurphu Dhondrup. Sitting: Phangdong Letsen, Dasang Damdul Tsarong, Depon Nyelungpa. Sitting front: Depon Tsogowa, Depon Surkhang, Depon Drumpa. 1920.

13. Left to right, standing: Unknown, Phuntsok Rabgye Ragashar, unknown, Doring Dingja Dorji Gyaltsen, elder Kyibuk Sonam Wangyal, younger Kyibuk Wangdu Norbu, Nornang Sonam Dorji, Major Penpa Tsering. Sitting: Shasur, Drumpa, Tethong Depon Gyurmey Gyatso, Laden La, Mondhong Kyenrab Kunsang. Front: Major Padma Chandra, Gokhar Sonam Gonpo. Early 1920.

14. Troops trained in the British military system parading in front of the Norbu Lingka palace.

15. The Drong Drak regiment. Photo by Spencer Chapman.

16. Depon Tashi Dhondup Yuthog and Datsap Jigme Taring, commanders of the new regiment called Drong Drak, the last effort of the Thirteenth Dalai Lama to revive the strength of Tibet's army.

17. General Dingja Dorji Gyaltsen is seen here reporting to the Commander-in-Chief and the ministers that the field-mountain guns that he and other officers brought with them after their training in India are ready for demonstration.

18. Left to right, sitting: Mr. W. H. King, an officer of the Indian Post and Telegraph Department; my father, D. D. Tsarong; Ngapo Shapé; Parkhang Dzasak. Standing: Kyibuk Wangdu Norbu; Mr. Rosemeyer, assistant to Mr. W. H. King.

19. This was the car that my father bought in Calcutta during his visit in 1924. We are at Dum Dum Airport. Left to right: The driver; myself, sitting on the lap of my nanny, Ani Chung Kyi; and in the back seat my aunt Mrs. Taring, and my mother. Partly seen at the back is Mr. Laden La's elder son, Willy Laden La. Sitting on the car step are Kula and Cuckoo and the younger son of Laden La, Pat Laden La. Standing at right front is Mrs. Laden La.

20. The new Tsarong house built in 1926, as it appeared in 1944.

21. The Choegyal Khang, the ceremonial hall of the Tsarong house, showing the life-size images of three early religious kings of Tibet.

22. My father, D. D. Tsarong, cracking jokes over the microphone at a party. Next to him is Mr. Chang Ngopa who had been sent to England to be trained in electrical engineering.

23. D. D. Tsarong at the same gathering.

24. My sister, Kunsang Lhakyi Shatra, our father, D. D. Tsarong, and myself in Calcutta, 1940.

25. Left to right: myself, His Holiness the Maharaja of Sikkim, and my father at Gangtok, Sikkim, 1940.

26. My wife, Yangchen Dolkar, and myself.

27. My wife and myself standing on the Trisam Bridge, 1942.

28. Kusho Tsumo Tsering Dolma, my father's youngest sister, and
my wife, Yangchen Dolkar, 1943.

29. Left to right: My mother, Pema Dolkar; my wife, Yangchen Dolkar; myself; and my father, D. D. Tsarong, 1943.

30. Left to right: Mr. Brooke Doland; D. D. Tsarong; Mr. F. Ludlaw, in charge of the British Mission in Lhasa; and Ilya Tolstoy, 1943.

31. My parents and myself when I was recovering from my fractured arm. The Sikkimese doctor Bo Tsering is next to me. The photograph was taken by Doctor Tennant.

32. D. D. Tsarong rafting on the lake at Lukhang behind the Potala Palace, 1944.

33. My father using his skill in photography. Picture taken by Heinrich Harrer, 1944.

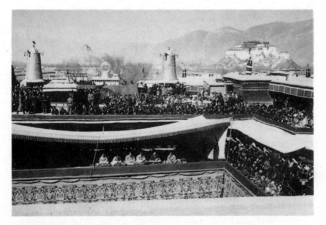

34. The Potala Palace as seen from the central temple, Tsuklag Khang, Lhasa.

35. My father and myself at the time of inviting His Holiness the Fourteenth Dalai Lama to the Monlam Chenmo in 1946.

36. My father and myself proceeding to the central temple, Tsuglak Khang, to offer our gratitude and thanks to His Holiness the Fourteenth Dalai Lama with gifts.

37. Myself walking over the suspension bridge built by my father in Drikung
Zongshol, 1946.

38. Front left to right: Peter Aufshnaiter, D. D. Tsarong, Tsepon W. D. Shakabpa, and Heinrich Harrer, who were inspecting the newly proposed hydro-electric site, 1948.

39. Left to Right: Tsedon Thubten Tsenlek, Mr. J. E. Reid of the General Electric Co. of India, my father, D. D. Tsarong, Peter Aufshnaiter, and Mr. R. N. Fox, who were responsible for the new hydro-electric proposal, 1948.

40. The first section of Trisam Bridge, completed in 1936. The remaining old sections were still standing.

41. My father and his colleague, a Chinese officer, and the staff of the newly formed construction department, which was closed down shortly after His Holiness the Dalai Lama returned to Lhasa from India in 1957.

42. Demonstraton by the people of Lhasa during the 1959 uprising against the Chinese rule.

43. My father arrested by the Chinese after they had crushed the 1959 revolt by the people.

Dolkar: myself and Kunsang Lhakyi, who was born in 1923. We were both kept at Gyatso until the trip to Calcutta in 1924, after which we all shifted to the new Tsarong House in Lhasa. My mother's sister Tseten Dolkar, who had previously been married to the heir of the Horkhang family, suffered a loss when her husband died at a young age, leaving her behind with two small children. Because the young widow was a daughter of the Tsarong family, Father would often visit the Horkhang House to advise her in running the large household. In the course of these visits he fell in love with her and they married in 1923. Tseten Dolkar remained at Horkhang House after the marriage, and had one son and six daughters with Tsarong. Mother's younger sister, Rinchen Dolma, who had accompanied us to Calcutta and Nepal, stopped her schooling in Darjeeling and returned to the new Tsarong House, where she began to help my father. With her knowledge of both the Tibetan and English languages, as well as mathematics, she provided much needed assistance in Father's business responsibilities such as record-keeping and correspondence. In 1927, Father took her as his fourth wife and one year later she bore him a daughter, Tsering Yangzom. Tsering Yangzom stayed on at Tsarong House, although Rinchen Dolma was later to marry Jigme Taring, the elder son of the Raja of Taring, and became part of the Taring family.

In all, Tsarong had ten children by three different wives, all daughters of Tsarong Shapé. The practice of polygamy was not unusual in Tibet. According to Rinchen Dolma Taring, the Tsarong sisters never felt any jealousy towards one another; families were kept separate and everyone was treated with equal respect. Tsarong took great responsibility for all his children. He saw the importance of a western-style education and sent several of them to the high-standard British schools in Darjeeling. Although not all of his children chose to attend, the opportunity was offered to all, boys and girls alike. His support was also extended later to his grandchildren, his brother's children, and even the son of our chief cook. His belief in education greatly benefited his children, especially his daughters, for later when they became refugees in India, they were remarkably self-sufficient and found productive careers.

Tsarong was renowned for his fiery temper among the officers and government officials, but he was also affectionately regarded by his children and grandchildren as a caring, loving man. It was hard to imagine that the Tsarong who so fiercely defended His Holiness and Tibet against the invading Chinese was the same man who, at night, would gather all the little children under his long woolen cape and tell bedtime stories until they fell asleep. It was clear that my father had many sides; most notably he was a man of great self-discipline. He ran a strict household and although he enjoyed drinking a brandy occasionally before retiring at night, he disapproved of drinking in excess. He also forbade any gambling at Tsarong House, despite the great popularity of *mah-jong* and the traditional Tibetan dice game, *sho*, in Lhasa.

By the late 1920s, the Dalai Lama was becoming more careful to examine the administration of the Government. He had heard from many sources negative information regarding the past functioning of the Kashag, and doubts of their loyalty were created in his mind.

At the Palace stable there were about forty grooms, called *chipyoks*, and His Holiness used to send some of these men to Lhasa to visit tea stalls, places where people gathered to discuss the news of the country. On their return to the Palace, they reported to His Holiness what they heard from the people. One day, the ex-general of the bodyguard, Kungo Surkhang, came to a tea stall that the *chipyoks* regularly visited. Officials from the upper class usually do not frequent street-side tea stalls, but he had a peculiar character and could mingle with anybody, anywhere. In the early 1940s, I once met him on the street, wearing an overcoat and riding a mule, alone, without any servant accompanying him. I did not know where he was heading, but it was an unusual scene. His character was similar to my father's, who also mingled with any class and who had no hesitation in doing menial work. What Kungo Surkhang was telling his friends in the tea shop that day was how he had been dismissed from his post, and considered himself lucky not to have been sent on service to Kham (eastern Tibet). This was eventually told to His Holiness, and soon Kungo Surkhang was sent to eastern Tibet on service. However, this was, in fact, exactly where he wanted to go. He went and did excellent service for the Government, taking part in the signing of the treaty between Xining and Tibet, and later becoming the Governor General of Chamdo. After his return to Lhasa, he was appointed Foreign Minister.

It was well known that the functioning of the Government was under much scrutiny as the Dalai Lama seemed to have lost faith in his cabinet ministers. The important papers that were sent to him for approval were very much changed in their content, many parts having been replaced with his own opinion in red ink. The Dalai Lama's corrections were always done in red ink, while others did not have the privilege of using this color. Often when names were submitted for consideration for specific appointments, they would all be rejected, His Holiness's personal choice being entered in red. The Kashag and many among the officials were well aware that His Holiness was rather disappointed with the administration of the Government and the behavior of various groups in the establishment.

One time, at a certain function during Nechung Oracle's Day, the Oracle had advised that the time had come to offer a long-life prayer to His Holiness. So the Prime Minister, the Kashag, and the Lord Chamberlain visited His Holiness and said, "We, representing the monks and laymen of the country, have come here to request Your Holiness to accept our prayers for your long life and seek forgiveness if we have made any mistakes on matters relating to the Government's administration."

In response to this, His Holiness gave his last testimony, in which he described in detail how he had dedicated his life to the welfare of his people, mentioning his two exiles and the fight for the survival of the country. He included in this testimony advice that the most important thing for Tibet was to have friendly relations with its two powerful neighbors, India and China. Tibet must have a strong defense with a well-trained army equipped with modern weaponry, powerful enough to withstand the challenges from the border areas. Without a defense force, the country would not survive. At present, His Holiness said,

Tibet is at peace, and it is in the Government's hands to work hard for the development of the country. If it continues to act irresponsibly as it has done in the past, disaster will fall upon the country. It will then be too late to repent. He continued, saying that it was well-known that this had happened in Outer Mongolia, where the Communists banned the search for its religious leader, Jetsun Dhampa. Likewise, when such an enemy encroaches on our land of Tibet, all incarnate lamas, including the Dalai Lama, Panchen Lama, and others, who are the defenders of the Buddhist faith, will perish. All nobles, monastic establishments, and government officials, and people from all walks of life will completely lose their freedom, along with their land. They will be oppressed by the enemy and remain under constant fear throughout the days and nights.

He concluded that as he had reached the age of fifty-eight, everyone should understand that his taking of responsibility was limited. He expected that the present peaceful situation would continue during his lifetime, but in the future loomed the danger of Communism. Now was the time to install protection against such dark days. This is briefly what His Holiness said in his testimony. The full text was published at that time and distributed by the thousands. It was also published in books, including a translation in the English language.

In 1931, the Government established a new mint at Drapshi. The Dalai Lama's intention was to make a large building complex, including a mint for the production of Tibetan currency notes, silver and copper coins, and postage stamps. There was also a building for the manufacturing of rifles and ammunition, as well as a large warehouse to which the Government armory was moved from the Shol armory below the Potala Palace. As Drapshi was becoming an important establishment, army barracks were built to accommodate a large number of troops. A new elite force of one thousand troops was recruited and increased in number until 1933. Kunphel La, a trusted favorite of His Holiness, was appointed, together with my father—who had much experience both in military and civil service—as heads at Drapshi. Depon Tashi Dhondup Yuthog and Datsap Jigme Taring were acting commanders of the regiments. They were also closely related to the Tsarong family. This renewed enthusiasm for strengthening Tibet's defense reflected His Holiness's testimony to the Kashag.

Despite the years of negative criticism and innuendo, had there been doubt in His Holiness's mind regarding the loyalty of my father, he never would have appointed Tsarong and his relatives to command this important establishment at Drapshi, which included the mint, armory, a military regiment, and military stores. These appointments clearly illustrated the trust which was ever-present between the Dalai Lama and Dasang Damdul Tsarong.

On the inauguration day, the Dalai Lama came for the opening ceremony. I went to Drapshi especially to see the arrival of His Holiness. From the rooftop of my father's quarters, I saw clouds of dust rising in the far distance near the sand dunes along the road. These were some of the bodyguards who were to be present when the Dalai Lama arrived. Outside the building, the full regiment was lined up in their newly made uniforms. His Holiness's yellow Dodge car appeared from the distance, and I went running down to watch the events. While the Dalai Lama passed, people were not allowed to watch from the rooftops, so I came down to the door and peeped through a hole. A little later, my father and Kunphel La appeared in the courtyard, followed by His Holiness with his attendants. Both men assisted him up the stairs to the main office.

Tsarong worked at the mint throughout the year 1932; in the summer of 1933, he was stricken by dysentery and a stomach ulcer. Medical treatment at Lhasa did not help him, so he applied for medical leave. Three months' leave was granted, and his plan was to go to Gyantse where he would consult the British doctor at the fort where the British trade agent was posted, and then visit his estate at Tsarong.

On the day of departure, he went to the Norbu Lingka Palace to take leave. His Holiness was kind enough to ask him to stay for lunch while the family members waited at Kyitsel Luding Temple. My father told me that during the serving of the lunch, Kunphel La came with table napkins and all but threw them on the Dalai Lama's lap. Father thought it was a highly disrespectful gesture, and it made him sad and annoyed. Kunphel La left for the Drapshi office. Afterwards the Dalai Lama suggested that Father join him for a stroll on the rooftop. Father said that His Holiness looked rather distraught that day. He looked towards Drapshi through his binoculars wondering how the project there would turn out.

Father took leave with a sad feeling. This apparently was their last meeting. Father then joined us at Kyitsel Luding, and we continued our journey. My mother, Pema Dolkar, myself and my sister Kunsang Lhakyi were with him. On our arrival at Gyantse, he got medication from the hospital, and we remained at Gyantse for about six weeks. Rest and medication did a lot of good for him. He had previously planned to send me and my sister off to a school in Darjeeling, India, and had asked His Holiness for his advice on which of the two schools, St. Joseph's College or St. Paul's School, would suit me best. His advice was St. Joseph's College. My sister and I were to leave for school in time for the new term, beginning in March.

As we had plenty of time left before our departure, Father decided to take us all to his estate at Tsarong. He was feeling much better, and we all enjoyed the peace and quiet of the estate. There we had a chance to visit the Tsarong Men-gon, a medical temple that was situated not far from the main house. The family of Tsarong is said to have descended from a long line of famous physicians who served both the Dalai and Panchen Lamas many years ago. This two-storied temple, dedicated to the Medicine Buddhas, was a very old and sacred shrine. At that time, eight monks were residing there conducting prayers and taking care of the daily offerings. In the main house, Father and I spent some time opening up many of the locked cupboards; although this was our estate, we had no idea of some of the things that had been stored here over time. We came across many very old medical instruments and books, which were very interesting. There were also the more typical items such as pocket watches, porcelain cups, silver cup holders and lids, etc. Father kept a few items with him, but most of the things he carefully replaced and locked up again. Of course we have no idea what became of all these things once the Chinese took over.

After several days, we traveled to a nearby hot spring and stayed for two weeks. The waters of this spring were very beneficial for good health. It was cold but sunny, and there were many children and relatives providing good company. By the end of six weeks, everyone was well rested and ready to move on. On our return journey we planned to stay for a period at Lhanga estate near Shigatse, which is two days from the Tsarong estate.

On the first day of our journey a special courier sent by my aunt, Mrs. Delek Rabten, arrived carrying a message to Father stating that His Holiness the Dalai Lama had passed away. He was shocked by the news and so overwhelmed that I saw him weeping for the first time. There was a small temple nearby where we stopped for the night, and he prayed and made offerings at the temple. We left the next morning for Shigatse and stayed at the House of Delek Rabten, my aunt's home. Father stayed here for a week preparing more prayers and offerings at the Tashi Lhunpo Monastery, which was only three miles away. We then left for Lhanga estate, which was situated on the bank of the river. One has to travel up the river and through Shigatse town, then down the other side to reach the estate. Just a mile after leaving my aunt's home, my horse suddenly climbed up the side of the embankment of a field, and I fell with the saddle to the ground. Although it was a short fall, and the ground was sandy and soft, my left elbow was dislocated. Everyone got down from their ponies to help because I was unable to get back on mine by myself. I was taken to Shigatse, which was not far away from the spot where I fell. At Shigatse, friends called for a Tibetan doctor who tried to put my elbow into position, but the pain was unbearable. I cried and asked Father to take me to Gyantse for treatment. After a second try by the doctor, he found he could not help; we then left again for the estate. We stayed there for one night, while preparations were made to take me to Gyantse by carrying me on a temporary stretcher with a hood on top.

As urgent arrangements had been made, Dr. Tennant, a British doctor who was stationed with the British Trade Agency at Gyantse, and his assistant, Dr. Bo Tsering, were already there when we arrived at the Dak Bungalow. They visited me every day, and after a few days they called Father outside the room and told him that my arm had to be put into the right position and that this would require that some force be used. The doctor recommended that I be given chloroform for the procedure. There was no option but to agree to whatever the doctor advised. The next day, my elbow was put into the right position, and when I woke up from the anesthesia, there was a great pain in my arm. In the afternoon doctors came and loosened the bandage with which my arm had been tied up tightly against my chest. Days passed and it was time for Father's leave to expire, so he made an application to the government for a further three months' leave of absence, which was approved.

My arm was still not functional, so going to school was out of the question. Father sent my two sisters on to Darjeeling without me. My mother went with them, and until she returned we waited at Gyantse. Together we then left Gyantse for home, and upon our arrival at Chushul, a special messenger sent by my Horkhang aunt was waiting. The letter advised that the situation in Lhasa was very turbulent and that Tsarong should delay his return for a while.

The period following the passing away of His Holiness the Thirteenth Dalai Lama was one of great social and political unrest. The religious community in Lhasa was busy performing the numerous duties and ceremonies that traditionally follow in this situation. Meanwhile, the various political factions were preoccupied with the many questions surrounding the Dalai Lama's death. Apparently, he had only been sick a few days with a flu, when his personal physician, Amche Jhampa La, gave him Tibetan herbal medicine; still His Holiness's health showed no signs of improvement. As the condition became more serious, the Kashag was informed. Kunphel La, who was the "trusted favorite" at that time, had great faith in the Nechung Oracle. Although he was only a fourth-rank official, his opinion carried a lot of weight, so Kunphel La called on the Oracle who, while in trance, prescribed another medicine to be given. Upon hearing this, Amche Jhampa La highly objected, stating that this particular medicine was too strong for His Holiness's current condition.

Both Kunphel La and the Oracle decided to go ahead regardless, and by the next evening the Dalai Lama had passed away.

As a result of his involvement, there were many accusations against Kunphel La, who was head of the new Drapshi complex along with my father. Simultaneously, a National Assembly meeting had been called to discuss the nomination of a Regent to take control of state and religious affairs until a new Dalai Lama was found and came of age. Many expressed the desire to elect a lama, but there were some monk officials who supported Kunphel La for the Regency. As Kunphel La was then a controversial figure in the political arena, many factions were working to suppress this appointment.

There was talk among higher officials that, in order to lessen Kunphel La's power, the elite military force at Drapshi (by then over a thousand strong) must be disbanded. Thus it happened that the Drong Drak, the Drapshi army troops, consisting mostly of sons of the middle and higher classes, were incited to desert. One evening, the troops rushed to Norbu Lingka Palace and declared their resignation, despite gallant attempts by Depon Yuthog and Datsap Taring to dissuade them. The men all went home to their families in Lhasa and never returned to the barracks at Drapshi. As Drapshi was then left without any protection, the Kashag and senior officers decided to send half the troops from the Norbu Lingka bodyguard unit (approximately two hundred and fifty soldiers) to guard this important complex.

Meanwhile, the inquisition into the death of His Holiness continued. Amche Jhampa La was called before the National Assembly to describe the events leading up to the death. At first, Jhampa La gave a simple explanation, but when it was rejected, he was forced to tell in detail what had happened. The Nechung Oracle was questioned, but the medium claimed ignorance, not remembering anything that occurred while he was in trance (which is often the case with mediums). The Nechung medium was then dismissed from his position; there would be no Nechung Oracle until the reception of His Holiness the Fourteenth Dalai Lama at Lhasa in 1939.

Finally, Kunphel La was summoned before the Assembly. He entered the meeting proudly, keeping his hat on his head. He was immediately scolded for his manner and looked upon in disfavor by the majority. Eventually, a verdict was reached and Kunphel La was taken from his residence at Norbu Lingka and arrested. He was then deported, along with his father, to Dema Chapnag Monastery in Southern Tibet. Later on in the 1940s, Kunphel La would escape through Assam to India with another favorite of the Thirteenth Dalai Lama, Tashi Dhondrup, who had been deported to the same area. Kunphel La settled in Kalimpong, West Bengal, for several years, and it was there that he met Tsarong and informed him of all the events which had occurred while Father was away in the south. Kunphel La returned to Lhasa after amnesty was proclaimed on the occasion of the enthronement of the Fourteenth Dalai Lama.

Later, my father told me that he was fortunate not to have been in Lhasa during the time of His Holiness's illness. He said he would certainly have rushed to the Norbu Lingka immediately and tried to give him aspirin for the fever, and perhaps would also have been blamed for the misfortune that followed.

Adding to the general political instability of that time was the need for the government to appoint a suitable regent. Different factions were rallying to have their candidate chosen and this created an atmosphere of tension and mistrust. Some time later, Tsepon Lungshar, then an outspoken figure in the government, was accused, along with his supporters, of planning drastic reform within the administration. He was caught fleeing from the National Assembly meeting where he had been convicted of treason and was placed under arrest in the Shol prison below the Potala Palace. As further punishment his eyes were to be taken out. Thus it happened, and he remained there blind in prison until general amnesty was granted by the Fourteenth Dalai Lama.

News of these events, along with warnings from family members, caused my father to reconsider returning to Lhasa. As he still had time on his leave, he decided we would all embark on a pilgrimage to southern Tibet.

At Chushul, the Kyichu River of Lhasa and the Tsangchu River merge, forming the Brahmaputra, which then runs into India. So we took a boat from Chushul south to Samye, a distance of about forty miles. We stayed at Samye Khencho's residence as his guests. He was the medium of the Samye Oracle and was close to the Thirteenth Dalai Lama, giving my father and him much in common to talk about from the past. We stayed in tents for the next ten days visiting the Oracle's temple and Samye Monastery, where Father made special prayer offerings. He visited all the other places which were considered highly sacred. Our camp had very pleasant surroundings, a wooded area with a stream running on one side and many birds of several species. I thoroughly enjoyed staying at Samye. The Samye Choejé, the medium, used to join us for every meal, and at breakfast time he used to come with a parrot in his hand and a pet sheep following him. When he gave the order, the sheep would lie down near the entrance. The parrot would perch on his shoulder and remain there while he ate.

We then left for Lhasa via Gyama, an estate belonging to my Horkhang aunt. She, along with her son and daughter, were already there when we arrived. They probably delayed their journey in order to meet us there, bringing with them the latest news from Lhasa. After staying a fortnight, we all departed together, journeying by boat from the nearest point of the river ferry. We arrived safely at our home after a twenty-five mile boat journey on the Kyichu River, which brought us within walking distance of Tsarong House. My father told me much later that had I not injured my arm, he probably would have returned to Lhasa as originally planned and would most likely have gotten caught up in the tumultuous situation at that time.

6 Public Works and Political Intrigue

It was sometime in June 1934 that we settled back into Tsarong House. Lhasa had experienced much disturbance in the past several months and the atmosphere in the city was tense. Father still had about a month left on his leave, so he had some time to rest and adjust to the current situation. In July, the first Chinese mission since the 1910 invasion was allowed to enter Tibet to offer condolences and prayers for the departed soul of His Holiness the Thirteenth Dalai Lama. It was led by general Xuang Mu-sang as the official representative of Chiang Kai-Shek's Nationalist Party. They arrived in Lhasa bearing many gifts and kind words, but it soon became evident that they had more than one agenda. During a ceremony the General awarded all the Tibetan officials with "medals of honor," which were engraved with the likeness of Sun Yat-sen, the great reformer of China. The Tibetans were quite alarmed by this action as it alluded to China's suzerainty over Tibet. They were not given as gifts, but as awards issued down from a higher authority. The Kashag was disturbed and not sure how to react. They approached Tsarong for advice. After some thought, Father suggested that the Kashag, in turn, should award all the Chinese officers in attendance with official Dzasak and other government uniforms, according to their ranks! This was then done, sending the clear message that the Tibetans considered themselves to stand on equal ground.

It was about this time that my father began thinking about the construction of modern bridges, as he was constantly having ideas of ways to improve Tibetan life. There was a wild river at Trisam, located on the main route to India and western Tibet. The Trisam River is about ten miles from the capital and it used to be a great barrier to travelers, taking lives during the rainy season. Thus it became a tradition among the local people to invite the Gadong Oracle, who would bless the old wooden bridge and often throw a golden ring into the water as a token of his blessing. Despite this, when the summer rains started, the bridge was washed away almost every year. Thus every year the villagers were burdened with the work of repairing the bridge, and sometimes, depending on the extent of the damage, they had to replace it completely and hope it stood throughout the next summer.

Aware of this situation, my father made a proposal to the government that he help to construct a modern steel bridge. It was approved, and he received a sanction for the construction. The manufacturing contract was given to Burn & Co., Calcutta. The fabricated steel structures were carried by men under great hardship across the Himalayas. The time consumed in bringing the materials was much greater than the time taken in the actual construction work itself. Throughout the construction period, Father lived at the site, initially in his tent, then later occupying quarters which were built for the officers and staff. He had Jigme Taring assist him during the construction. With his understanding of plans and drawings, Jigme's skills proved to be of great service to my father. Mr. J. Thaisong, who had worked as a personal driver to His Holiness the Thirteenth Dalai Lama, was also very helpful. He had been trained as a motor mechanic in Calcutta, and also had experience in building construction.

The first section of the bridge was completed long before the rainy season of 1936. When my sisters and I came home from school for our winter holidays, we were surprised to see the progress, and we were able to ride on Tibet's first steel bridge. The middle section was completed in 1937 and the last section in 1938. At the time of completion there was an opening ceremony, which the Regent Reting and his ministers came from Lhasa to attend. It was a great feat in the history of Tibetan bridge construction and the Regent offered scarves and gifts to congratulate Father and the rest of the construction staff. The river was no longer an obstacle for travelers, and there were no more fatal accidents for the thousands of men and animals that passed over it.

Great hardships were suffered by the peasants in the district where the new bridge had been built, and while my father was in the district, the Government asked him to look into their difficulties, that is, to investigate the heavy loans that burdened the people of that area. He accepted the task and at the end of a long and tiresome piece of work, he managed to get consent from the creditors to forego the interest that had been accruing for many years. He also arranged for the principal amounts to be paid in installments. When the people of nearby districts heard that my father had been successful in persuading the creditors to write off the heavy interest charges, they appealed to the Government for similar investigations to be made in their own districts. The Government again appointed my father to take up these matters. Although the work was exceptionally wearisome, he was always ready to help people who were suffering from the burden of their loans.

While investigating loans in other districts, he discovered another difficult obstacle for travelers: a dangerously narrow path on the cliff of Jang, which is about twenty-two miles from Lhasa. The road led up a steep cliff, below which the Kyichu River runs, and loaded animals often fell into the river. My father made his suggestions, and a plan was sanctioned for the construction of a road along this river so as to avoid the dangerous climb along the precipice. He supervised construction during his loan investigation work in this district. A safe, wide road was built along the river by elevating the riverside with large stonework. It was a delight to every traveler.

In 1939, His Holiness the Fourteenth Dalai Lama arrived in Lhasa. We children were at school in Darjeeling at that time, so Father made arrangements with the school for us to leave one month earlier than the scheduled winter holiday. We arrived at Lhasa early on the morning of the Dalai Lama's arrival. After changing our clothes, we went straight to Dogu Thang, a very large field where the welcoming reception was to be held for His Holiness the Fourteenth Dalai Lama. All government officials of every level were present. In fact, they had arrived there a day earlier, resting for the night in their tents. It was the custom to make a large camp of tents for the occasion. The tents were pitched around the Dalai Lama's reception tent and the other tents for his personal use; all of these were enclosed by a curtain of white, heavy cloth which acted as an outer fence.

There was a grand procession when the Dalai Lama reached Lhasa. The procession included all government officials, as well as representatives of the monasteries, various artisans, tailors, and military units. When His Holiness neared the Tsuglak Khang, the Nechung Oracle came out in trance, wearing his elaborate costume to welcome him. After a brief visit to the Temple, the procession continued to the Potala Palace.

Throughout the year of 1939 my mother was ill. Many doctors had been consulted, but she became increasingly weak. She was stricken with a complicated stomach illness which at times caused great pain. When an attack occurred, the only cure was to give her morphine injections, which she received for a long period. Needless to say, my father was devoted to her and spent much of his time supervising her treatment. There were always a number of relatives and household servants present to assist.

One day, Rai Bahadu Norbu, who was then in charge of the British Mission in Lhasa, came to meet Tsarong with his Sikkimese doctor, Rai Sahib Thonyoe. The doctor advised Father to take Mother to India for medical treatment without further delay. Father immediately made the decision and applied for leave from the Government. Late in December we left Lhasa; Mother was accompanied by Father, my sister, and myself, and Rai Bahadu Norbu was kind enough to send Doctor Thonyoe with our party.

As Mother had to be carried in a palanquin, we could not move very fast. Instead of the usual double stages, we could make only one stage per day, and so it took almost a month to reach Gangtok, Sikkim. Three days into the march, just a few miles before reaching our house at Chushul, Mother suffered another attack. Doctor Thonyoe, myself, and two servants rode ahead to prepare the injection, and when Mother arrived and received the injection, the pain subsided. During the anxious days of our long journey, we tried to cheer ourselves and Mother too. Thereafter, she had no more serious attacks, only minor ones which were controlled by oral medicines.

The day we reached Gangtok, the then Maharaja of Sikkim, Sir Tashi Namgyal, had sent both his car and private secretary about five miles up the Nathula Pass to receive us. During our three days' rest at the Palace, we were the guests of His Highness the Maharaja. We then left for Calcutta, where Mother was admitted to the School of Tropical Medicine. The x-ray report revealed that she had gallstones and, as she was becoming very weak, the doctors recommended immediate surgery.

During our stay in Calcutta, which lasted over a month, we had nothing to do except visit Mother in the hospital. Father had time to spare, so we traveled to various places of interest in Calcutta. A month and a half later, Mother became quite well, and we left for Darjeeling for further medical treatment and convalescence. After a gradual recovery of her health, we prepared for our journey back to Tibet.

The family happily returned home to Lhasa, and a vast number of relatives and friends came to meet us. As was the Tibetan custom when returning home after a long absence, one had to call on all one's relatives and friends and distribute presents. This is done in order to return the generosity, in the form of gifts, which one received before departing. It also serves to reestablish contact with the community. Father had purchased many presents in India for these calls.

During the time we were away in Calcutta, His Holiness the Fourteenth Dalai Lama was ceremonially installed on his throne. There was a grand procession from the Norbu Lingka Palace to the Potala, and everyone lined the route to catch a glimpse and receive a blessing from the new Dalai Lama. Although he was officially enthroned on that day, he was only five years old, and the Regent would assume all political power until His Holiness came of age. Tsarong, on his return from India, called on Regent Reting, who was a young reincarnate lama of Reting Monastery, and who had been elected as the Regent in the absence of a Dalai Lama. It was on this formal call that the Regent expressed his desire to visit our home. Father thought it

was a great joke because there was no precedent for a Regent to
visit a private home, but the subject was brought up repeatedly
during conversation. One day Tsarong received an invitation
from the Regent for a lunch, and I was told to accompany him.
We went to Reting Labrang, which was his residence. After lunch,
he announced that there would then be target shooting with .22
caliber rifles, and added jokingly that today was the day that he,
the Regent, was prepared to compete with a famed military man.
Tsarong suggested that since he had not handled a rifle for a
long time, his son, as a younger man, should instead take up the
challenge. The Regent then suggested that a day's party be arranged by the loser. Father agreed, and stated that if his son were
to lose, as probably he would, then he would have to bring the
cook for arrangements to be made here at the Regent's residence.
The Regent replied, "If your son loses the game, you will arrange the party at your home, and I shall come."

It must have all been prepared beforehand because the rifle
and target were suddenly ready at the Regent's command. The
target was placed in the garden, and we were to shoot from one
of his rooms on the third floor. Of course, I lost the competition
because he had prior practice on the same range and was accus-
tomed to his own rifle. So the party was to be arranged at Tsarong
House, and Father suggested that the time should be in the month
of July, when our garden would be at its best.

The day of the Regent's visit was fixed for July, 1940. All members of the family and servants were at the gate to receive him,
while I was standing by with my movie camera to record this
rare visit. The Regent came with his brother and other attendants, numbering about ten, including his advisers. Father led
the party to our reception room where the Regent was shown to
his seat on a throne that had been carefully prepared. Ceremonial tea and rice were served. After that, Father offered a welcome scarf, and thereafter members of the family offered their
scarves and received his blessings. Once this simple ceremony
was finished, the Regent got down from his throne and took a
seat near the window on a sofa. More tea was served. After talking for some time with Father, he went around the house inspecting some of the rooms. Then he was taken down to the
garden where he sat on a swinging chair. He was delighted to

see the garden; that year was the best season we had ever had. A special lunch table was prepared for him, and others, including Father, were seated on leopard and bear skins that had been spread on the ground, giving the atmosphere of a picnic. After lunch, Father had organized games including target shooting, which was the Regent's favorite sport. Although he loved rifle shooting and practiced often, the sport was restricted to targets only. In Tibet, the shooting of any animal is prohibited by religion.

Another of the games they played was passing a soft ball, trying to hit one another. Once my father had the chance of hitting the Regent, which everyone took as a great joke, as no one had ever dared to hit the Regent during his lifetime. It was all great fun, and I took many pictures that day. A lavish afternoon tea was served in the garden, after which everyone went into the house. The Regent sat again on his throne, and Father performed a simple ceremony by offering him a scarf. Gifts were also presented as a mark of respect and thanks to him for visiting the house. Tibetans believe that it is a great blessing to receive a high lama of his position into one's home, and thus one should show much gratitude. The Regent then left, and, as was done when he first arrived, the whole family went out to the gate to bid him farewell.

❀   ❀   ❀

During Tsarong's time as head of Drapshi Mint, he had brought out the new paper currency of one hundred *sangs*, twenty-five *sangs*, ten *sangs*, and five *sangs*; silver coins of ten *sangs*, three *sangs*, and one and a half *sangs*; copper coins of five and three *sho*; and postage stamps of four *tam*, two *tam*, one *sho*, and *kar chegyey*. Apart from his duty at the mint, he had to attend the National Assembly, which is called whenever there were important state decisions to be made. During the Regent Reting's reign, Tsarong was offered the post of Cabinet Minister (Shapé), the same post he held in the 1920s under the Thirteenth Dalai Lama, but now he politely declined.

From 1940 onwards, the work at the mint was seriously hampered because of frequent failures of the power supply. The equipment at the power station was wearing out, causing frequent work interruptions. On the occasion of His Holiness the Dalai Lama's entry as a student into the three great monasteries, Drepung, Sera, and Gaden, the Government, in consultation with the Finance Ministry, had decided to bring out a new issue of twenty-five *sang* currency notes. As the Drapshi power station was inoperable, there was hardly any time to complete the work. Father asked me whether the power could be supplied by the ten horsepower diesel engine that I was importing for our home lighting. I replied that it could definitely power the printing machines, and I would be delighted to offer its service. The engine was being brought from India and it was then en route not very far from Lhasa. The Government made special calls and it was brought to Drapshi within a few days. In the meantime, I consulted with Mr. R. N. Fox, who was working at the Indian Mission in Lhasa; he was using the same size engine to power the Mission. It was my first experience working with diesel engines, but with the guidance received from Mr. Fox (who later joined the service of the Tibetan Government), the work was done and the currency notes were completed on time.

Tsarong knew that constant repair of the old machines along with the use of a small diesel engine would not be adequate for the future needs of the mint. He decided to propose a scheme for a new hydroelectric power station to be imported via India. Here again, Fox's guidance was requested. He advised that as the roads across the Himalayas were narrow and precipitous, importing heavy equipment was out of the question. It was therefore proposed to purchase three 125 kilowatt hydroelectric generating sets from England (Gilbert Gordon Ltd.). These were much lighter than the higher capacity machines.

Soon work began on the civil engineering side of the hydroelectric project through the employment of Mr. Peter Aufschnaiter, who was a survey engineer. Peter Aufschnaiter was an Austrian who escaped to Tibet from a prison camp in India, along with his companion, Mr. Heinrich Harrer, the author of *Seven Years in Tibet*. Their indomitable courage had brought them to Lhasa after risking their lives on numerous occasions. In the early months of 1946, when we heard that two white men had arrived in the city and were encamped in the courtyard of the Lhasa electric substation, Father told me to go meet them. My wife and I went with some food and provisions, and on our return I reported their condition to Father. The next day he invited them to come to our house to stay, and they remained with us for a period of almost two years. Consequently, they became our good friends and performed various jobs for the Tibetan Government. Peter escaped from Tibet when the Chinese Communists overran our country. He later worked for many years with the United Nations in Nepal.

Aside from his work at Drapshi, Tsarong was less active in governmental affairs than he had been in the past, though he still kept well informed of the political situation. While attending meetings as a member of the National Assembly, he continued to offer suggestions aimed at both improving the lives of the Tibetan people and bringing the country forward into the international arena. At one point Father made strong suggestions to the Kashag that it should consider opening Tibetan consulates in foreign countries. This would certainly amount to some expense, but he thought it very important for international relations. The Kashag, however, was ambivalent.

Father also had a personal interest in stamps and stamp collecting. In the late 1940s, he approached the Kashag and requested that Tibet join the International Philatelic Society. Although the membership fee was only a few *do-tse*, again the Government showed little enthusiasm. Father was not discouraged, however, and he continued pursuing this interest on his own. There was an American, Mr. William Englesmann, who had written to Father requesting Tibetan stamps, and this began a lifelong postal friendship between the two men. Having such divergent cultural backgrounds, they had plenty of interesting information to exchange. Englesmann was an industrialist from Missouri and sent Tsarong many *Life* and *National Geographic* magazines, and other Western publications, which our whole family enjoyed. My father in turn sent Tibetan gold rings and jewelry, *thangkas*, and once he even posted a carved Buddhist altar, such as those kept by Tibetans in their prayer rooms.

Englesmann and my father never met in person, but in 1961 on my first visit to the United States, my wife and I traveled to

Missouri to meet him ourselves. He and his wife welcomed us kindly into their home, and, as he was showing me around the house, he proudly brought me to what he called the "Tsarong Room." Upon opening the door, I could hardly believe my eyes; the things which Father had sent him over the years were all beautifully displayed about the room. What a surprise to see so many Tibetan things there in Missouri, at that time! It was extraordinary how two men who had never met had touched each other's lives from so far across the world.

Towards the end of 1940, the Regent Reting summoned the Kashag to tell them that he wished to take leave from his office for a period of three years. It is common for monks and Rinpoches ("Precious Teachers") of the Tibetan Buddhist tradition to enter a three-year retreat at least once in their lives. As the responsibilities of the regency were immense, after seven years in office, Reting Rinpoche wished to take leave to concentrate on his religious studies. This, he added, was to be carried out according to his horoscope and the advice of his lamas. The ministers strongly requested him to continue his reign until the Fourteenth Dalai Lama came of age to take over administration of the country. The Regent was adamant, and paid no heed to their request. He recommended to the Government that Takdhak Rinpoche, the senior tutor to His Holiness, become the regent in his absence. Takdhak was approached, and he accepted the position, entering the regency in January 1941. Following the completion of his three-year retreat, Reting and his supporters wanted to come back to power, but Regent Takdhak remained in office, ignoring their demands. After failing in all their peaceful efforts to gain control, they attempted to seize power by forceful means. The Regent Takdhak and the senior members of the government discussed the situation in an emergency meeting, which led to the call for the ex-Regent's arrest.

In February 1947, two ministers, accompanied by other government officials and two hundred and fifty soldiers, went to Reting Monastery to arrest Reting Rinpoche for suspected treason. This incident angered the Sera monks of Jhey College, who strongly supported the ex-Regent. The monks had charged the army procession in an attempt to rescue Reting Rinpoche while he was being taken to the Potala Palace. However, owing to lack of force, they failed to free him. The monks then began a series of raids on houses in Lhasa, searching for arms and ammunition. This caused severe panic in the city, and, as we had many rifles in our house, we thought ours would be one of the likely targets.

During this time, Father was away from home. He had been requested by the people of Drikung District, some thirty miles away, to build a small suspension bridge. Tsarong had a very strong relationship with the Drikung Kagyu monastery, which began during the time of His Holiness the Thirteenth Dalai Lama's reign. Chetsang Rinpoche was a close relative of the Thirteenth Dalai Lama, and as Tsarong was constantly by the Dalai Lama's side, he formed a close bond with the Rinpoche. Monks from Drikung often frequented Tsarong House, seeking advice regarding administrative affairs of the monastery which involved the Tibetan Government, and Father was always happy to offer suggestions and assistance. Even after Drikung Rinpoche passed away in 1943, Father maintained a steady relationship with the regent and the monastery. When it became evident that the Drikung District was in need of a new bridge over their local river, Tsarong did not hesitate to go there and oversee the project. It was during this period that the arrest of Reting took place.

We sent four armed servants with a detailed letter explaining the situation and asked Father to return immediately from the Drikung District. We realized we now had only a few men in the house, and if any raiders came, we would have no defense at all. So I called our two Austrian friends, who were staying in one of our guest houses, and we discussed a strategy. We brought out all our rifles and found that we had more than were needed. After searching in the storerooms, I found a damaged Lewis gun with its stand, and we placed it conspicuously on the roof, so that people would hear and see our display of arms. We then placed torch lights around the rooftop which gave the impression that many people were present and defending the house. Fortunately, the incident passed without disturbance, but the city remained tense and people were constantly on guard. After a two-day journey, Father returned from Drikung with his armed servants accompanied by many others sent by Drikung Monastery as escort.

The National Assembly was continually in session during the ex-Regent Reting's trial; Tsarong had to attend the meetings for many days. The assembly was held in the Potala Palace, and Reting, who had been brought from his residence, was locked up in the Potala. I was then serving in the Cabinet Ministers' office as a secretary and had to remain at the Potala for a number of days. The ex-Regent was brought for trial before the Assembly many times and admitted all the details of the conspiracy planned by his supporters to overthrow Takdhak Rinpoche and take control of the Regency. The Assembly took pains to decide what punishment would be possible for a man of such position as a high Rinpoche who was involved in these serious political issues. When a proposal to slice off the calf muscles of the legs (a common punishment to disable the guilty party) and other similar punishments were discussed, Tsarong and my father-in-law, the then Commander-in-Chief Ragashar (officially known as Dolkar Shapé), strongly opposed it. Tsarong suggested to pass the sentencing on to the Regent Takdhak Rinpoche, who would settle on a punishment. Being a reincarnate lama, it was expected that the Regent, from his deep understanding of compassion, would make the sentence more lenient. In the course of further discussions, the ex-Regent unexpectedly died in prison, creating certain doubts in the minds of many people, as he had been perfectly healthy at the time of his arrest. The death of the ex-Regent Reting made it easy for the Assembly to complete its work. All those attendants and supporters who were found guilty were punished with life sentences in prison or public flogging, depending on the level of their involvement.

❀　❀　❀

In addition to his work for the Government, Father had many responsibilities at home. At Tsarong House he cared for my mother, Pema Dolkar, as well as my sister and myself. In 1938, Father's wife Tseten Dolkar, widow of Horkhang, passed away from complications after childbirth. Some time later, many of the children from Horkhang House came to live at Tsarong House where my mother cared for them as if they were her own.

By the 1940s we were coming of age, and I was one of the first to get married. My wife, Yangchen Dolkar, was the daughter of Dolkar Shapé and a long time-friend since childhood. In 1942 my sister Kalsang Lhakyi was married to Shada Gaden Paljor. Gaden Paljor's grandfather, Lonchen Shada, was the plenipotentiary of the Tibetan Government at the Simla Convention in 1913. My elder half-sister, Tsering Yangzom, was married to Jigme Dorji, son of Raja and Rani Dorji of Bhutan House.

The system of marriage in Tibet during this century differs in many ways from that of old times. The old, traditional custom was that a child's marriage was arranged by his or her parents. The young people may or may not have met each other prior to these arrangements; definitely there was no courtship before the marriage took place. In later years, parents openly discussed the marital arrangements, and the boy or girl could reject the proposal if it was not to their liking. Traditionally, once an internal agreement is finally reached, high lamas and an astrologer are consulted to determine if the couple is suited or not. The proposal is then relayed, by a common friend of both houses, to the bride's home, along with a ceremonial scarf. This scarf has the special function of signifying whether the proposal was accepted or not. Acceptance of the scarf meant that the proposal was agreeable to the parents, and it was only in rare cases that the marriage would later fall through. When everything was finalized satisfactorily, the groom's house selected an auspicious date according to the astrologer's advice on which a representative from his house, along with his party, would arrive at the bride's house to draw up an agreement between the two families. The bride's parents and relatives also attended the ceremony. Ceremonial scarves were exchanged with the guests, followed by rice and tea, which are considered auspicious foods. The agreement was then read by the representative of the bridegroom, and the seals of both houses and witnesses were affixed. The agreement was written in a standard form, except for the beginning, which was finely expressed in poetic verse, as was the style of many official documents of those times. After this ceremony, the guests were entertained, and then returned to the bridegroom's home to report the success of the meeting.

The final day for the wedding was chosen by again consulting astrologers, who would discover an auspicious date by making astrological calculations based on the birthdays of both the bride and bridegroom. Two or three days before the wedding day, representatives of the groom and his servants, arrayed in their best costumes, would leave for the bride's home, where they were received ceremoniously. They were well looked after by the house, and parties were arranged every day. The wedding day ceremony would begin very early in the morning, usually before dawn, so the bride's party had to arrive at the groom's house long before sunrise. Her party included the representative and a host of servants from her home and the people from the groom's home who came to escort her. The long procession would ride to the groom's house, where they were first met by a group of people from among whom a woman in her best costume offered a silver bowl filled with *chang* (local beer). After the bride dipped her finger into the *chang* and tossed some drops into the air in an offering gesture, the procession continued. They would meet the second reception outside the gate, and the same performance would be repeated. The third reception was in the courtyard of the house before the bride dismounted onto a specially prepared platform. The platform was made by stacking up sacks of barley to form a base about forty-one inches square and fifty-one inches high, which was covered with five-colored brocades and a tiger skin spread in the center. The bride dismounted onto this platform with the aid of servants and then she was led into the house. On top of the staircase of the house, the groom's mother would await the bride and greet her with a bunch of keys, which was then handed over to her. This signified that she now belonged in that house.

The bride would first visit the chapel to pay homage to the house deity, a symbol of allegiance to the house. She was then led to the ceremonial room, where all the members of the family would be seated. A separate seat was made for the bride and groom facing in the appropriate direction as specified by the astrologer. Tea would be served, followed by rice and yogurt, which are all considered auspicious food items. The head servant of the house would enter with his assistants and offer congratulations and scarves to everyone in the room. A group of servants, who had been trained previously in ceremonial song and dance, performed their acts. Tea would be served again, and the ceremony was over. The bride and bridegroom would then go to the roof, where a shorter ceremony was held. Here, the representative of the bride's house would bring out a flag acquired especially for this purpose. Holding the flag in his right hand, he would announce the marriage and make a commendation of the flag, after which he placed the flag alongside the other flags on the roof. These colorful flags are printed with holy writing and can be seen flying from the rooftops of many Tibetan homes.

At this point, there would be a break when everyone would change from their ceremonial clothes to more comfortable suiting. Soon the members of the bride's family would arrive and there would be receptions upon their arrival. The bride's family usually stayed at the house for many days. A stream of visitors would come to congratulate them with gifts and scarves; they would be received by the bridegroom only. For many days after, parties continued for the members of the two families and the visitors who came to congratulate them on the occasion.

The 1940s were a time of marriages at Tsarong House. Most of Tsarong's children were married in those years except for my half-brother, Phuntsok Gyaltsen. He remained single and worked for the Government until his arrest by the Chinese during the uprising in 1959. He was then deported with roughly 120 other officials to a Chinese prison somewhere near the Mongolian border. Somehow he managed to survive these circumstances and, after eighteen years, he and nineteen of the original prisoners who had survived along with him were released. He resumed his life, eventually married, and had two sons who now live in India.

Along with the marriages came the births of Tsarong's many grandchildren. Father adored his grandchildren; no matter how busy he was, he always found time to be with them, especially in the evenings when he told them bedtime stories, which they loved. As he did with his children, he insisted that his grandchildren all have an equal opportunity to go to the British schools in Darjeeling, and many of them did. Between 1942 and 1949, my wife and I had our five children, two daughters and three sons, and four of them went on to finish their secondary schooling in Darjeeling.

My second youngest son, who was born in 1946, was recognized as the incarnation of Drikung Chetsang Rinpoche, one of the two heads of the Drikung Kagyu lineage. As mentioned, even after the passing of his friend, the previous Drikung Rinpoche, Tsarong kept a close relationship with that monastery. It so happened that as administrators and attendants of the previous Rinpoche came to Tsarong House to discuss different matters, my son, at the age of only two years, exhibited an unusual attraction to these monks. He constantly wanted to be close to them and when they left, he wished to go away with them. The monks of Drikung were highly observant of this and noted his actions carefully. They began occasionally dropping by Tsarong House under false pretenses, without calling on the parents but simply asking the servants to bring the young child out to play. Eventually he was put to several tests to which all candidates for recognition as reincarnate lamas are subjected, namely identifying among many objects the specific ones which belonged to the previous incarnation. After reviewing all the candidates and consulting the master astrologers, as well as the Takdhak Regent, who had final word, it was decided that my son was indeed the true incarnation of Drikung Chetsang Rinpoche.

As the predecessor was his close personal friend, Tsarong felt very pleased having the incarnation born into his own family, and of course my wife and I were quite surprised as well. My wife Yangchen does not remember any special incidents during the pregnancy, but there were some auspicious circumstances regarding his birth. Close to the time our child was due, preparations were being made for Drukpa Tseshi, an annual holiday celebrating the day Lord Buddha first taught, or "turned the Wheel of Dharma." On this occasion all Buddhists go on short pilgrimages to sacred places in Lhasa. It is felt to be a highly auspicious day and, therefore, the Takdhak Regent decided to offer a full set of new ornaments to the image of Jowo Rinpoche at the Tsuglak Khang. Jowo Rinpoche is a sacred symbol of the Lord Buddha, but is also believed by many to be more than just a symbol. It is regarded by most Buddhists of Tibet and neighboring countries to be one of the most sacred images in existence. The Regent must somehow have been aware that Tsarong was in possession of a beautiful eighteen-carat diamond that he had purchased in India on one of his many trips. He sent his close friend Tsepon Shakabpa to our home to request that Father sell it to him. Shakabpa explained that they were in need of a very precious stone to be the centerpiece of the ornamental headdress they were offering to Jowo Rinpoche on Drukpa Tseshi. Father agreed and sold it at cost.

Days later, my wife went into labor and after twenty-four hours, the baby still had not come. We were fortunate to have the assistance of Dr. Guthrie from the British Mission in Lhasa. Everyone became concerned as the labor was so prolonged. Strangely enough, many hours later, on the auspicious day of Drukpa Tseshi, during the precise time at which the ornaments were being offered to Jowo Rinpoche, our son was finally delivered. He was born not breathing, and most of the relatives gave up hope that he would live, but through the perseverance of Dr. Guthrie who, confident in his skills, slapped and tossed the baby about, his breathing finally started.

About three years later, our son was formally recognized as Drikung Rinpoche, but because of his young age, he remained at home with the family until 1950. At that time, the Regent and representatives of the Drikung Monastery came to Tsarong House to fetch Rinpoche. He was brought back to Drikung Monastery in a ceremonial procession and officially took the seat as successor of the Drikung Kagyu lineage.

Tibet was at peace when most of the world was experiencing the turmoil of the Second World War; however, our country did not go unaffected. Slowly interaction and trade with foreign countries began to increase. When Japan invaded Burma, the Allied powers' military supply line to China was cut off. China sent a team of surveyors to eastern Tibet with the purpose of constructing a new route through that area, but as they had no permission, the Tibetan Government stopped them from entering. A new military supply line by air was then started from India to Kunming, China, crossing a corner of the southern border of Tibet on through the Himalayan mountain peaks. It was a treacherous route where many accidents occurred, and was referred to as "the hump." It was not only dangerous, but very expensive in both men and materials. In fact, several planes were lost flying over this hump. Many Tibetans will also recall that in August, 1944, one plane flew over Lhasa and crashed somewhere near Samye, about thirty miles to the south. Miraculously, all five crewmen parachuted to safety and, with the assistance of the local authorities, made their way to Lhasa. The Tibetan Government looked after them, and after a few days' rest, they journeyed to India on horseback.

In the summer of 1942, the President of the United States, Franklin D. Roosevelt, sent two emissaries, Captain Ilya Tolstoy and Lieutenant Brooke Dolan, to negotiate a road transport of supplies to China. In the course of their stay at Lhasa, Tsarong met them on several occasions and came to know them well. One day, Captain Tolstoy mentioned to Tsarong that he and Lieutenant Dolan would like to make Tibetan seals for themselves, and they asked Tsarong to suggest appropriate Tibetan names for the seals. Father gave the name A. Damdul, meaning "Victorious over Enemy" to Tolstoy and A. Kalsang, meaning "Auspicious Aeon" to Dolan. Adding "A" before each name stood for "American" and it is also a Tibetan word which is used to address a person given the status of an elder. The master engraver, Tsakpa Jhampa, made the seals, and they were much appreciated by the visitors.

As Tibet chose to remain a neutral country, it did not permit movement of military supplies to China by land; however, permission was given for the transport of civilian goods. Soon after this permission was granted by the Government, the trading of goods in large quantities commenced. Several Chinese businessmen came from India bringing their wares for distribution in China via Kunming. These goods included jeans, various cotton materials and other textiles, cigarettes, indigo dye, and many other commodities. Everything could be sold in Kunming at a good profit.

The Chinese traders would exchange their Indian rupees—which they had in large quantities in the Indian banks—for Tibetan currency. The traders needed the Tibetan money for their payment of transport from Lhasa to Kunming. So Father acted as a banker and supplied them with Tibetan currency; he did a profitable business in this way. Other houses in Lhasa also did similar business. Eventually, Tibetan traders began to send goods to Kunming and also became quite successful. However, at the end of the war, many traders suffered great losses because the value of the Chinese dollar quickly dropped to almost nothing. The Tibetan currency, however, remained very strong throughout the war years.

Tsarong had an excellent business sense, even from his youth, and as there were no restrictions against government officials conducting their own private business, Father took advantage of the opportunities which were there. In the 1940s his business flourished; like the Chinese, he had sent large numbers of mule and camel caravans to Kunming. He traded in cigarettes from India and tea from Burma (which originated in Yunnan Province), as well as Tibetan wool and animal skins. He also did a fair amount of importing goods to Lhasa. From India he imported textiles, cigarettes, edible oils, and some precious stones like coral and turquoise. Overall it was a prosperous period in Tibet; the economy was sound, the export of wool had reached its peak, and the amounts of other exports had also increased to a record high.

Father was able to greatly increase the wealth of Tsarong House during these years, and as he was a man of tremendous generosity, he never failed to share this prosperity. Actually he exhibited altruistic motivations all his life. As a young man, while traveling through Mongolia with the Thirteenth Dalai Lama, Tsarong had established an export business through a local shop in the capital city during his stay there. Speaking Mongolian, he was able to form a close bond with the Mongolian people. Thus, whenever new Mongolians arrived in Lhasa, they almost always stopped at Tsarong House to be oriented to the city. Father set up his Mongolian trade in such a way that the profits would be extended to any young Mongolian monk who wished to pursue his religious studies at one of the great monasteries of Lhasa. A few years ago, my daughter, Mrs. Namlha Takla, was approached at her home in Dharamsala by an elderly Mongolian scholar who praised the generosity of her grandfather. It was through his business in Mongolia that the scholar as a young boy had been funded to travel to Lhasa and study at Drepung Monastery, where he stayed for many years, eventually traveling to India to accept a teaching position. Many stories such as these have been related to family members by those who were assisted by D. D. Tsarong.

As Tsarong prospered from his own business, he was also helpful and encouraging to others who wanted to start their own businesses. He was by this time quite knowledgeable about the trade routes and the cultural ways of India, so many men came to him for advice and assistance in getting started. Although Father did not always benefit, and often lost money in these start-up investments, it did not seem to bother him. He was a great source of energy and was always looking for opportunities to put his resources to use. As a Buddhist, he was inclined towards supporting religious institutions, and many monastic communities benefited from his kindness.

In the mid-1930s, the Karma Shar Oracle was in need of some assistance. The House of Karma Shar was an old Tibetan establishment dating back many centuries. It was the residence of the Karma Shar Oracle, to whom many Tibetans from Lhasa and elsewhere came to make offerings in order to appease the deity. Once every year there was a ritual dance performance during which the Karma Shar Oracle would go into trance and give predictions. Many different dances were performed by a professional troupe of fifty to sixty dancers. The costumes were beautiful and very elaborate, but after many years of use they had become overly worn. Because of their close relationship, Tsarong came to know of the situation and volunteered to refurnish the entire troupe with new costumes. It was a big expense, but Father valued these dance performances, as they were believed to appease the Oracle, and to help in this way was highly meritorious. Thus, he was happy to be able to provide this support.

Father was also one of the patrons of Tsangpa Khangtsen, one of the houses of Drepung Monastery. There, several hundred monks resided, and whenever they needed guidance or advice in some matter, they would often come to Father. Twice a year, Father would organize a lengthy prayer offering to be held in the Choegyal Khang at Tsarong House. In the spring there would be a recitation of the entire Kangyur and Tengyur—the complete collection of Buddhist sutras and tantras—which was 108 volumes. Every autumn, the Dolma Bum-ther—the 100,000 prayers to the Goddess Tara—would be performed. Approximately thirty monks would be invited from Tsangpa Khangtsen to recite these prayers, and it was customary to serve them excellent meals, as well as Tibetan butter tea, almost continuously throughout the day. The service lasted about two weeks, and at the end, all were richly rewarded for their efforts. It was a good occasion to have these prayers performed as it brought merit to the family and household members, and my parents were happy to sponsor such events.

According to Tibetan custom, it is appropriate for one individual or family to officially invite the Dalai Lama to the annual Monlam Festival, which occurs after the Tibetan New Year. The invitation must be issued one year in advance, as there is much responsibility and preparation involved. However, there is also great merit in such an undertaking, as one ideally sponsors such a ceremony for the welfare and benefit of one's country and family, as well as one's self. In 1946 Tsarong had invited His Holiness to the Monlam, which is held at the Tsuglak Khang temple. Although it was not until February, preparations had begun months before. As the date approached, the work increased, and many servants and family members were engaged to help. I myself, along with Robert Ford and Mr. Fox, organized the lighting system with a petrol engine. There were hundreds of offerings to be acquired, organized, and wrapped for presentation. Some of these included quantities of grain such as barley and wheat; butter; salt; silk brocades imported from China and India; tiger, leopard, and bear skins from Tibet; a pair of huge elephant tusks with exquisitely engraved solid silver bands, which were imported from India; and solid silver-offerings in the shape of horseshoes. There was also a monetary offering of five hundred *do-tse*, and each *do-tse* was individually wrapped. Tsarong had also engaged 250 monks, each of whom was to carry two *do-tse* in the offering procession to the Tsuglak Khang. Most of these monks began arriving at one o'clock on the morning of the festival. Of course, our family was up all night taking care of last-minute details.

Two days before the day of the festival, it is required of whoever has invited His Holiness that year to go to the Potala and officially invite the Dalai Lama to the Monlam Chenmo. On that day, Father and I went together to the Potala Palace to extend the invitation. We then escorted His Holiness in a large procession from the Potala to the Tsuglak Khang, where he remained in his own private residence located above the great prayer hall. On the day of the actual offering, once the gifts had all been delegated to the appropriate carriers, we again proceeded to the temple in grand procession in our finest clothes.

Family members, along with the government officials were seated in the balcony of the prayer hall, while the monks (over twenty thousand in attendance) were assembled on the main floor. Father and I went up to the Dalai Lama's residence and the Donyer Chenmo announced that we had arrived. We then led His Holiness down to the main hall, carrying burning sticks of incense before him. It is an elaborate ceremony with various age-old customs and rituals in which it is both an honor and a pleasure to partake. Once offerings and prayers are completed, everyone disperses. Father and I then led the Dalai Lama back up to his residence and at that time our family was granted a special audience in his private reception room. At this time, officials offered us ceremonial tea and rice, and we each offered His Holiness a scarf and received his blessings. It was a majestic affair that brought my father great personal satisfaction, and was a memorable event for everyone in our family.

❀   ❀   ❀

In October 1949, after the Communists took full control of China, Radio Peking announced that the People's Liberation Army would liberate Tibet and Taiwan. This type of announcement soon became a daily routine over the air, disturbing the minds of the peaceful Tibetan people. The Tibetan Government was alarmed by the news, and the National Assembly was often called to discuss the situation. Tsarong, still a member of the National Assembly, was attending these meetings. In the summer of 1950, Chinese troops began sporadic attacks in the eastern border areas. In October, the Communists attacked Tibet in full strength from several different directions. As the citizens of Lhasa began to fear what was to come, many men, especially those of the noble classes, sent their women and children to India. At first my mother, sister, and other relatives departed, then shortly after, my wife and four of our children left for Kalimpong, West Bengal. Kalimpong was a favored place at that time as a hill station not too far from the border (only a sixteen-day journey from Lhasa) and as a main trade center between India and Tibet; there were plenty of vacant houses to lease and many friends and relatives who were settled there.

The Government agreed that, although he was still young, His Holiness the Fourteenth Dalai Lama should take charge, so on the seventeenth of November, the Regent Takdhak stepped down, and His Holiness assumed full temporal power. One month later, as it became apparent that the situation was becoming worse, the National Assembly requested the Dalai Lama leave the capital for Dromo, a Tibetan town on the border of India. On the nineteenth of December in early dawn, the Dalai Lama and his party departed, following the main road, while Tsarong along with a few officers and myself were instructed to follow the route along the southern side of the Kyichu River. We also left at dawn, and when we camped that first night, using our binoculars we could clearly see His Holiness's camp across the river about four miles away. The next morning, we again left early in order to be on the left side of the moving party. Unlike the Thirteenth Dalai Lama's flight in 1909, Father traveled on the left of the moving party as a precautionary measure, even though there was no definite danger of pursuing forces. The southern side of the river was considered at risk from a possible swift outflanking by Chinese Special Forces before the Dalai Lama could reach his destination.

On the fourteenth day after we left Lhasa, we finally arrived in Dromo. It was a memorable morning. That evening, the Dalai Lama and his party arrived safely. Tsarong made his camp at Rinchen Gang, four miles further down toward the Bhutan border past His Holiness's camp. This was a big junction from where the road leads up to both the Nathula and Jelep La passes, as well as being a main route to Bhutan. During His Holiness's stay at Dromo, circumstances forced him and his ministers to make many decisions which eventually led the Tibetan Government to agree to send representatives to Peking for negotiations.

7 Flight and Return

The decision of His Holiness and the Tibetan Government to return to Lhasa was made after the so-called Seventeen-Point Agreement was signed in Peking. Soon after this decision became known, a Chinese advance party headed by General Chang Ching Wu arrived at Dromo, via India. Upon his arrival, General Wu became very upset because the Dalai Lama and his ministers did not come to receive him as the representative of the People's Government of China. He was, however, received by a group of senior officials of Tibet's Government. The following day when General Wu was informed that the Dalai Lama would meet him at Dongkar Monastery, Wu insisted that His Holiness instead come to Dromo. Dongkar Monastery is about four miles from the town of Dromo, where the Chinese General was encamped with his staff. After some debate about the meeting place, the General finally agreed to come to the monastery to meet the Dalai Lama. His Holiness the Dalai Lama afterwards left for the capital city.

Tsarong and the Foreign Minister, Surkhang Dzasak, were sent ahead of the Dalai Lama's party. My mother had traveled up from Kalimpong to accompany her husband on his return journey to Lhasa. My wife remained in Kalimpong, and when the new term began, she enrolled our three eldest children in school in Darjeeling. I also remained behind in India on government duty, buying and shipping electrical equipment back to Tibet. Father spent an extra day at Gyantse and stayed at a house named Changlo, an estate belonging to Yabshi Phunkhang, where he had a strange experience. He had a dream in the early morning that a man with a short beard on his chin was begging Father to save his life. It was so clear a vision, yet Father could not understand its meaning. When Mother woke up, he told her the dream. After breakfast, they strolled on the roof towards the front of the building and saw that people were busy putting up seats in the courtyard; a higher seat in the middle and lower seats on both sides. A fireplace was built in the center. My father then asked the people what was happening. He was informed that the estate manager had died earlier and his spirit was haunting the area and had caused trouble in the house, so they were preparing an exorcism. My parents watched the performance and while the monks were chanting, a woman was brought into some kind of trance with the help of others. She was made to kneel down before the fire, and when the Lama threw some barley grain in the fire, she screamed as if she had been hit by it. This was repeated a few times, and eventually she fainted and was carried away by assistants.

When I returned after several months in India, my parents related this story to me. I described a certain man's features and Father exclaimed that the man in his dream was exactly like the one I had described. He was surprised when I said it must have been Shango Pothang. Father asked who he was and how I knew him.

I told him Shango was a servant of Phunkhang who used to accompany Phunkhang's children to school. I knew him quite well, but, as many years had passed, I had no idea of his whereabouts. Later I checked with friends in Lhasa, who confirmed that this servant had indeed been appointed manager of Yabshi Phunkhang's estate near Gyantse and that he later died at that place.

The Dalai Lama returned to his capital on the seventeenth of August, 1951, and, as usual, most of the people in Lhasa turned out to welcome him. In a grand procession, His Holiness proceeded to his summer palace, Norbu Lingka. On such occasions, every official, both lay and monk, would join the procession in ceremonial costume. The roadside was lined with people, some burning incense, others with ceremonial scarves in their hands. There were also dancers in their costumes and monks holding religious symbols and banners in their hands. Some Chinese who were with General Chang Ching Wu's party witnessed the scene, and I can imagine that it must have been with great amusement, for they would never have experienced such a scene before in their lives.

In September 1951, the first Chinese troops, numbering about three thousand, arrived in Lhasa under the command of General Wang Chi Mey, who had come through the usual main route to Lhasa. They were followed by another force of three thousand under Generals Tang Kuo Ha and Tan Kun San, who had followed the northern route.

They used every available transport; a great number of camels and mules were loaded with their army supplies. In spite of a transport shortage, they managed to bring with them a U.S. Army jeep that had been dismantled and carried by camels. On the day of their arrival, it was assembled and driven alongside the troops. The long column of soldiers was led by their cavalry, carrying five-star red flags. On either side there were several groups of dancers in peasant costumes. Their faces were painted red, they wore red clothes, and everything on them was red in color. So, when some of the people who watched the Chinese arrival were asked later at home, "What were the Chinese like?" they answered, "Their faces are red and everything on them is red." The elders who remained at home replied, "Then they must be the real Red Chinese." Tibetans did not really know what Communism was; they were a peaceful and religious people who never bothered learning about the outside world. Tsarong had witnessed the arrival of the Chinese army, and he had the opportunity of taking several photographs that day. With several thousand Chinese troops already in the city and the constant arrival of Chinese in civilian clothes, the price of every commodity soared to a height unheard of in the past. Chinese soldiers began collecting bones for their cooking fuel, the burning of which polluted the air with a horrible smell.

The greatest obstacle the Chinese had to face in Tibet was the language barrier. They had come to a strange land whose language and culture were totally different from their own, and they encountered a great problem in communication. In order to solve this problem, adult schools were established, and Tibetan teachers were hired to instruct the Chinese in the Tibetan language.

At the request of the Chinese, the Tibetan Government supplied grain, temporarily solving their food shortage. When these supplies were exhausted, the Chinese resorted to other means of getting food, namely tapping the grain supplies from the monasteries and private estates. This was cleverly achieved by inducing the Tibetan Government to set up an office for collecting grain and money on "loan" from private estates that belonged to the monasteries and officials. The office was named Drukhang Lekhung, meaning "Office of the Granary." The officers to whom the work was assigned were specially chosen for maximum effect. These men were from the monasteries, aristocracy, and other prominent citizens, among whom Tsarong was one of the senior officials. When the first meeting was held, the Chinese officials laid down their "suggestions," stating that the committee members themselves should first agree as to how much each member could contribute before calling on outsiders. This put everyone in an embarrassing position, and the meeting ended with a suggestion that the members could first check their personal records before making a final commitment. Under the prevailing situation, with the capital occupied by thousands of Chinese troops, the committee members thought that a small contribution would not satisfy the Chinese and that a substantial amount of money and grain should be offered. So in the following days, the members made large contributions for which they were issued receipts. Later these receipts became meaningless scraps of paper. Father had to attend these committee meetings for several months.

Tsarong had retired from the Finance Ministry the previous year, so he had not much to do except attend the traditional ceremonies. He was still a member of the National Assembly, but there was no need now for the Assembly to meet. During this time, he was free to look after his garden and enjoyed his hobby of planting fruit trees. Apple, pear, peach, and plum trees had been imported from India years before, and eventually he propagated the young trees through grafting. Father was very successful in the grafting and budding of fruit trees. We had many fruit trees which bore enough fruit to send to relatives and friends, as well as for our own use. Even grapes were grown there in Lhasa, but in a glass greenhouse only. My mother's health was poor, so Father was glad to be at home most of the time.

At one time, Father decided that each grandchild should have their own tree, one that they themselves were responsible for planting and watering. My son Drikung Rinpoche has a good memory of spending time with his grandfather in the garden of Tsarong House. One day, when visiting from the monastery, Tsarong had his grandson plant a new peach tree that was about three feet in height. The child set about digging a hole at the chosen place in the garden. As his hands were small, it took several hours; Tsarong stood by and offered words of encouragement. As the tree was then planted, Tsarong and his grandson spent a moment of peace together admiring his work. About one year later, Rinpoche insisted on returning to see "his tree," and much to his surprise, it had already borne five or six large peaches! The garden was a great source of pleasure and satisfaction for Father—one he would not be able to enjoy very much longer.

In 1954, the Chinese put pressure on the parents of all Tibetan students who were studying in India to have them return to Tibet. There were about twenty at that time, my own children included. The Chinese claimed that they would receive a superior education in the Chinese schools in Lhasa, or even those in Peking, where many had been sent to study. My wife, Yangchen Dolkar, then went down to Darjeeling to bring the children home. Everyone was happy upon their arrival back at Tsarong House.

The Chinese were consolidating their hold on Tibet using two main highways: one that runs through the northern plateau and the other via the southern route. Many Tibetan officials and prominent people were taken to China on conducted tours. The Dalai Lama was also taken to China with the Panchen Lama in 1955. These yearly tours were aimed at indoctrinating the Tibetans into the Chinese culture; however, they mainly succeeded in depressing the morale of the people through displays of China's modern industries and especially their impressive military might. Tsarong was also asked to visit China, but as he was

122 of His Country

an aged person, he was excused from that hazardous trip. Each year hundreds of people were taken to the neighboring country as a matter of routine, until the Chinese realized that this tactic would never change the attitude of the Tibetans. Thus, the annual tours were cancelled after 1956. By early 1956, the situation in the east was changing for the worse. The eastern Tibetans, the Khampas, were revolting. In spite of the Chinese effort to suppress the revolt by sheer military force, the Khampa revolt spread into different parts of the country, even as far as central Tibet. Thousands of people were killed and refugees poured into Lhasa. The capital was flooded with rumors, causing great anxiety and suspicion among people in the Central areas. These warning signs later proved to be true indications of the events to come.

With the situation worsening in eastern Tibet, the Chinese Government exerted pressure on the Tibetan Government to set up the "Preparatory Committee for the Tibet Autonomous Region." The body was inaugurated in April of 1956. A fifty-one member committee was formed; the Dalai Lama was the chairman, and the Panchen Lama was vice-chairman. The method used in the selection of the members was the same as that used when the Granary Office was established. There were only five members who were Chinese; the rest were all Tibetans, but most of the members were pro-Chinese. Moreover, the basic policy was decided by the Chinese Communist Party. It essentially served as a local puppet government. Tsarong was one of the senior members selected from among the Dalai Lama's officials. In the initial stages, various departmental heads were appointed. Father was made the head of the Construction Department, along with a Chinese counterpart. The next stage was the procurement of an office building. My father was asked if he would help the Department by loaning part of his home. This was a gross encroachment of privacy, but in the prevailing situation there was no way to refuse. Many others who owned sufficiently large houses had fallen into the same plight. Father brought the news home and everyone, including the servants, was anxious and fearful. My mother's health was poor and the news of Chinese moving into our house caused her even greater anxiety. Within a fortnight, the whole of the ground floor and outbuildings were filled with Chinese. There was no end to the traffic in the court-yard: people, trucks, and mule carriages coming and going. The house became like an army barracks: whistles sounding in the early morning and people doing their morning exercises in the courtyard and playing in the garden. They washed near the well; water, especially soapy water, was thrown everywhere, regard-less of damage done to the trees and flowers. Everyone was frus-trated, yet we could do nothing. Still, we tried our best to be friendly with the visitors. The garden which was loved by all of us quickly deteriorated and we just watched it wither away.

Mother was once again becoming seriously ill from her stom-ach ailment. She had gallstones, and an operation could not be performed in Tibet. We were all anxious and busy nursing her, especially Father, who would look after her at night, when the attacks came. During the day, my wife, myself, and others nursed her as well. After a long period of illness, she recovered once more but was never truly happy because of the intruders living in the house creating disturbances throughout the day.

About the middle of 1956, Prince Thondup Namgyal of Sikkim arrived in Lhasa with an invitation letter for the Dalai Lama to attend the Buddha Jayanti celebration in India, which marked the 2500th anniversary of the birth of Lord Buddha. The Prince was the President of the Mahabodhi Society in In-dia, and he had come personally on behalf of the Society. The invitation was accepted by the Dalai Lama, but the Chinese suggested that a representative could be sent in his place. They said the Dalai Lama's presence in the capital was very impor-tant at that time because the Preparatory Committee for the Ti-bet Autonomous Region had just begun its work. The Prince waited in Lhasa for over a month, but no concrete decision was made as to the Dalai Lama's attendance. There was growing criticism of the Chinese when the people of Lhasa came to know about this. The Lord Buddha's anniversary celebration is con-sidered by all Buddhists as something very precious to their hearts, and hindering his visit was the worst thing the Chinese could have done for public relations. In India, there was great excitement over the forthcoming celebration; Buddhist cen-ters were renovated by the Government of India, and they were

expecting millions of people from all the Buddhist countries. Fortunately, the Chinese reluctantly gave in, but only after receiving
a formal invitation to the ceremony themselves from the Government of India. I believe the Tibetan people's voices also carried
great weight with the Chinese in making their decision.

Now that the Dalai Lama was free to leave, many Tibetans
also planned to leave for the celebration. Father could not go
because he was the head of the Construction Department, which
already had a great accumulation of work. I, too, was in the Construction Department, but since I was holding a job of lesser responsibility, I took leave for the celebration in India. Because of
the current situation, my wife and I realized that this might be
our only chance to move our children safely out of the country.
Under the pretext of joining the pilgrimage to India for the Buddha Jayanti Festival, my wife notified the children's teachers at
school. We did not discuss our decision directly with the children—if many people came to know, there might be problems
preventing a smooth departure. My parents took the news with
heavy hearts, as they were very much attached to their grandchildren, my mother especially. When my eldest daughter,
Namlha, was ill with typhoid, Mother nursed her and brought
her back to a full recovery. Likewise, my youngest son, Paljor,
was very ill when my wife and I left for the China tour in 1955,
and it was under my mother's care that he, too, recovered. Once
she realized that she might never see her grandchildren again,
she became very distressed and often talked about them before
we left Tsarong House. Although we never seriously discussed
our leaving home for the last time, Mother knew what lay ahead,
and it was difficult to be optimistic.

On the day of our departure, we said goodbye to our parents,
who were very sad, especially Mother, who had tears in her eyes.
When she bade farewell to the last child, I saw her leaning towards a cupboard and weeping. With a heavy heart and tears in
my own eyes, I pulled the door shut and left. My father-in-law,
being one of the cabinet ministers, accompanied the Dalai Lama
in his entourage, so my mother-in-law joined our party. We drove
for two days and reached Dromo. We then had to ride over the
Nathula Pass, which is the frontier between Tibet and India. On

reaching the top, I looked back into Tibet and saw the beautiful mountain Chomo Lhari at Phari, standing majestically among the vast chain of mountains. I took many photographs as I always used to do when the weather permitted. We crossed the pass at a leisurely pace and immediately began our decent. We were now in Sikkim and our party was happy and excited to meet our friends and relatives who resided there.

I was pleased to have been able to bring my children out of Tibet, yet my thoughts went back to Lhasa where my parents still were. Though we were walking downhill most of the time, we had saddle sores, so we were relieved when two jeeps sent by the Choegyal of Sikkim came to fetch us. Finally we reached Gangtok, happy after a successful trip.

After a three-day stay at Gangtok, we left for Kalimpong. We learned that the Dalai Lama was in New Delhi, and that he would be visiting all the Buddhist centers in India shortly. Soon we received our first letter from home telling us that everything was well there. A few days later, we left Kalimpong for the Buddhist pilgrimage centers, staying at various places for a day or two and listening to the news of the Dalai Lama's movements. We learned that the Dalai Lama had made a complaint to the Chinese Prime Minister, Chou En Lai, who happened to be in India, about excessive Chinese pressure regarding reforms in Tibet and other atrocities. There were also rumors that the Dalai Lama and his ministers might not return to Tibet until a satisfactory understanding was reached between Tibet and China.

Upon our return to Kalimpong, we found a great number of Tibetans—officials, traders, monks, and peasants. Some were returning to Tibet, others were waiting to see how the situation developed. His Holiness had, at this time, already decided to return to Tibet, and so most of the Tibetans left for home.

I remained in Kalimpong with my family and made arrangements for my children's reentry into Mount Hermon School in Darjeeling. Later on, my two sons Jigme and Paljor were sent to St. Joseph's College. Darjeeling is situated at an altitude of almost seven thousand feet above sea level, and it was because of the cool climate that the British established so many good schools and colleges there.

Sometime in April of the year 1957, I received a telephone call from Gangtok, Sikkim requesting me to come to the radio station there the next day to receive a call from my father in Lhasa. I reached Gangtok in time for the call. When the operator handed over the microphone, my father's voice sounded very low and hoarse, and he told me that Mother's health was again not so good; he advised me to come soon to see her. I immediately agreed and told Father that I would leave for Lhasa the day after next. I felt he was pleased to hear this. I drove back to Kalimpong immediately and started packing my suitcase for the journey. On the third day, I left Gangtok accompanying a group of muleteers who were making a trip to Dromo. We reached Dromo the next day, and I unsuccessfully tried to find a seat in a Chinese truck going up to Lhasa. On the second day, with the help of some friends, we found a new truck that was making its first trip to Lhasa. It was one of those that was brought up from India and reassembled at Dromo. We started the journey rather late; the driver was a Chinese man aged about fifty. After a few miles of climbing from Dromo, the weather became cloudy and windy, and I was getting rather cold in spite of my heavy fur coat. We began to smell burning oil coming in from the back of the truck, so the driver and I both got down, and we found that the rear axle was smoking. There was no oil in it, but fortunately the driver had brought some oil in a can. We continued our journey, and, after a long and cold drive, reached Gyantse late at night. The driver insisted that we remain an extra day at Gyantse to fix the truck. I was in a desperate hurry to get to Lhasa, but we were stuck because the truck was not serviced properly at Dromo. Anyway, we resumed our journey early on the third day. The driver and I did not speak a common language, and there was nothing that we could make each other understand.

On reaching Shigatse, the second largest town in Tibet, we still had about a hundred and fifty miles to cover before reaching Lhasa. We drove on the dusty road along the Tsangpo River. The midday sun was quite strong, and I felt very warm in the truck in all my heavy dress. Suddenly, I found the driver was dozing while driving, and I could not say a word because of our language barrier. The only thing I could do was continue to supply him with cigarettes and candy. Twice I steered the truck before it went off the road. Then we came to the ferry, and the truck was driven onto a wooden barge that ferried us to the other side. We continued our journey after a brief stop for lunch. The road then climbed up the mountain side, and the air became cool again. At least there was no more danger of my driver going to sleep, although I still kept supplying him with candy and cigarettes. We finally crossed the Shugu La Pass, which is about 15,500 feet, and reached Lhasa around six in the evening.

When I entered the gate of our house there was no one in sight, and I proceeded to the inner gate. I had expected many Chinese, full of activities in the courtyard, but to my surprise there were no Chinese to be seen. A servant coming over from his own house to the main building greeted me at the door, and he immediately told me that my mother was ill and that he was glad that I had come. While walking up the stairs, I asked him what happened to the Chinese. He said simply, "They have gone away." I then came to the room where my mother usually stayed and quietly opened the door and stepped in. I saw that she was lying near the window on a Tibetan-style bed-like seat, and my father and sister were there with her. They were all surprised to see me because there was no way to let them know that I would be arriving on this day.

My mother's health improved steadily, and in a month's time she had fully recovered. She had learned from my father that the Chinese Construction Department was in the process of moving to another place, and our house would soon be free to ourselves. I found that there was a somewhat more relaxed attitude among all the people whom I met. The Chinese had slowed down their policy of reforms, and many offices had closed for the time being. This must have been the result of the Dalai Lama's talk with the Chinese Prime Minister, Chou En Lai. However, in general, the country's situation was still precarious because a great number of Khampas, eastern Tibetans from Kham Province who had revolted against the Chinese rule, had been driven from their homeland by the Chinese forces. Several thousand of these Khampa patriots took to the mountains and continued to fight the Chinese by guerrilla warfare, leaving their wives and

children behind. They headed towards Central Tibet while continuing the resistance. Other Khampas left their homes in eastern Tibet, many with their families, and arrived in large numbers
at Lhasa as refugees. Within a short time, those men who had
come to Lhasa also took the southern road to join their kinsmen
in fighting, leaving their families behind as well.

During the course of my stay at home, I decided that I should
go back to India and return to Lhasa with my wife as soon as
possible, leaving our children in Darjeeling to continue their education. After a month's stay, I left for India again, driving my own
jeep this time. At the border town of Dromo, I left the jeep in the
care of some friends and hired some riding mules for the journey.
This time I had two servants who were accompanying me. We
were traveling in the best time of the year. The air was dry and
cool and we had beautiful weather throughout our journey.

Upon returning to Kalimpong, I went with my wife to
Darjeeling to see our children. For many days we had been discussing our return to Lhasa and leaving the children in school.
We did not know whether we would be able to come again to
India, or whether we could bring the children back to Tibet in
due course. Both our parents were in Tibet, and our children
were now at school in India, so it was difficult to make a decision. Finally, we agreed to leave for Tibet, and before our departure, we again went to Darjeeling to meet our children. They
had no idea of the severity of the situation, and we did not want
to worry them by discussing it. It was a sad parting; we did not
know whether we would see them again after a long time, or
whether we would see them again at all.

Shortly after our return to Kalimpong, where we were then
residing, we left for Tibet. As usual, our first stop was Gangtok,
Sikkim, which is only a fifty-mile drive from Kalimpong. My
wife and I stayed an extra day at Gangtok to prepare for our
return journey. Our riding mules and other pack animals were
sent ahead while we drove up in a jeep. My Indian friend Motilal
Lahotia had offered me the use of his jeep. Although he accompanied us, I drove the vehicle myself. The road was fairly good
for about ten miles, and then it became narrower, steeper, and

stony. We had learned that one or two other jeeps had made it another ten miles, and my friend insisted that I drive on as far as possible. The going was very slow, but we finally made it up to Tsongo Lake, which was our stopping place for the night. The next day it was cold and raining, and we bid farewell to Motilal, who then drove back down to Gangtok. We resumed our journey on horseback, still climbing for another seven or eight miles before reaching the top. The great Nathula Pass and its surroundings were very familiar, for I had crossed this way twenty-two times since my early school days. We now had to descend to about 9,000 feet, which was done in approximately four hours. We stayed an extra day at Dromo to prepare my own jeep, which had been left behind when I came down. We then drove out and reached Lhasa on the third day, glad to be together with our parents once more.

There were no longer any Chinese living at the house, and it seemed the same as before, yet the situation of the country was not at all good. There was talk in the city of the refugees from the east—soldiers, monks, and other patriots—continuing to set out from Lhasa to join the revolutionary forces in the south. Many among the anti-Chinese faction from Lhasa also left with them secretly. There was a great amount of fear and uncertainty behind the relatively calm manner with which we tried to go about our daily routines.

One day, after a month's stay at home, we were all outside having tea in the garden, when suddenly my mother became ill once again. Her usual stomach trouble had started, and soon we had to take her into the house. She became worse that night, and we had to call a Chinese doctor, who gave her a morphine injection that put her to sleep. She slept the night fairly comfortably, but when the effects of the injection had worn off, the pain in her stomach returned. The following day she was very sick and weak. There was nothing we could do except to sit with her in turn both night and day. On the third morning of this attack, the Chinese doctor came and gave her another dose of morphine to relieve the pain, but he said that the end had come and that she would live only a few more hours. The members of our family remained anxious, and some of us went to the Tsuglak Khang to pray. It was the evening of July 17th, 1957, that she passed away. We all knew that her time was near and she herself knew also. Fortunately, there was no pain, and she remained in meditation and prayer. Her words were clear at first, but soon became slurred and then ended with a single hiccup. It was a great loss to the family, especially to my father, who had lost his life's companion of forty-five years.

Tibetan funeral arrangements are rather elaborate, and mourning lasts for forty-nine days, during which continual prayers are offered by the lamas. Requests were made to the Dalai Lama and other high lamas and monks for special prayers to be said for the departed soul. Great charitable works were also done such as giving alms to the poor. This is a Tibetan custom, and it is our belief that such charitable work may help one's departed soul, as it may relieve part of the sin that might have been committed during one's lifetime and may even contribute to the enlightenment of the soul.

During her lifetime, my mother had worked tirelessly for the family. It was her responsibility not only to run the household, but also to look after the many children who lived there until they married and left home. Preparations for a Tibetan girl's marriage are extensive. As the bride leaves her own family and joins the family of the husband, her jewelry, clothes, money, and all the provisions she needs for her dowry and to continue her life in a new house must be organized. These traditional customs were followed for most of the marriages of Tsarong's children, with my mother supervising and making sure everything went smoothly. Arranging these marriage ceremonies in addition to running the household was a great responsibility, yet my mother found in them a great source of joy and satisfaction.

Months after mother's death, a silent sorrow still had not departed from our hearts. My father especially was very much depressed by the death of my mother. I tried to keep him company most of the time, and in my absence there were always one or two of my sisters with him. Numerous reports reached us of the revolt in southern Tibet, and rumors were spreading in Lhasa of imminent trouble. We tried not to inform our father of the disturbing news. In October, my wife left for India to fetch the children from school, as winter holiday starts in December. I suggested they take a leisurely pilgrimage to the various Buddhist centers around India: Bodh Gaya, Sarnath, Delhi, Agra, Calcutta, and other such places. Before she left, it so happened that our son Drikung Chetsang Rinpoche was visiting from his monastery. He was accompanied by his tutors and several attendants. My wife requested that they give permission for her to take Rinpoche to India so that he could join in the family pilgrimage. His tutors, however, would not allow it, as he was nearing the point in his religious training when he was to enter a three-month retreat. They felt that the time away would disrupt his program. So, sadly, my wife departed without him, arriving safely in India and continuing on a pilgrimage with a group of many relatives and friends.

Meanwhile, some of our men returned from the southern border. They went there to make arrangements for prayers at various monasteries, and they warned us that the situation in that part of the country was very grave. One day I mentioned to my father that it was customary to make pilgrimages to various sacred places, not only in Tibet but also in India, a country which is considered by Tibetans the sacred land of the Buddha. I suggested that it would be appropriate to make an application to the Government for a leave of absence in order to make an offering of prayers for the departed soul of my mother. At first he was skeptical about it, but later agreed with my idea. I then proceeded to see all the ministers, explaining our situation, and made formal applications for both of us. The Government was slow to make the decision, but finally granted the leave—for my father only. Father said that there was no point in going to India alone, and so he decided to go for pilgrimage within the country instead. However, I was not discouraged by the decision, and again I went to see the ministers to make another formal application. A leave of absence was then given, allowing me to go as far as the Tibet-Sikkim border to see my father off. I was satisfied with this and we immediately began making preparations for our trip. I began by giving a thorough checkup to the Land Rover, while waiting for our truck to return from the border at Dromo. There were no service stations in the city; all vehicle maintenance had to be done by ourselves.

We left on the morning of December 18th, 1957, leaving Tsarong House in care of my youngest sister, Thondup Dolma, and the household servants. Thondup Dolma was the only sister who had yet to get married. We progressed by short day trips, only stopping for extra days at both Gyantse and Dromo. Dromo was where the motorable road ended, and we then had to travel by horse. I made myself busy jacking up our car and draining out the radiator, etc. The next day we left Dromo and immediately began ascending the Nathula Pass. We were late in starting, so we stopped for the night at a small village about two miles away from the top of the mountain. The weather was kind; there had been no snowfall on the pass for many days. The sky was clear, spotted with countless shining stars, and we expected good weather for our crossing the next morning. We reached the top of the pass at sunrise, and we remained there for some time looking at the beautiful surroundings, drinking tea from our flask. I took several photographs. I had no permission from the Government of Tibet to go further than the border, but a sense of urgent decision arose in my mind. I did not discuss this point with my father, as it was obvious to him that I was going along for the pilgrimage. Since there was no one to stop me from going, I decided to cross the border with Father and send a cable to the Government as soon as I reached Gangtok. This I did immediately upon arrival.

Our next stop was at the Fifteenth Mile (as measured out from Gangtok), a small village where travelers and transport muleteers stop for the night. The next day, we were met by a jeep which was sent by my sister, who was married to the Prime Minister of Bhutan, Jigme Dorji. We did not stay at Gangtok for the night, instead driving straight through to Kalimpong, which is another fifty miles. We reached Kalimpong late that night, and were pleased to meet my wife, children, and sister, who were all anxiously awaiting our arrival. The children spent the rest of their winter holiday in Kalimpong; Father was happy to be reunited with his grandchildren.

After having a few days of good rest, we began meeting friends and relatives. My father was very glad to see his old friend Mr. David Macdonald, who had been the British Trade Agent at Dromo in 1909, and who had helped him to escape to India during the Chinese trouble that year. Macdonald was now retired, and his daughters were running the Himalayan Hotel in Kalimpong. There were several exchanges of visits between our friends for a few days. Then Father left for his pilgrimage, and my sister and I accompanied him. Prayers and offerings were made at all the sacred Buddhist sites, especially for the departed soul of my mother.

After our pilgrimage-tour in India, my sister returned to Kalimpong, and Father and I left for pilgrimage to Nepal. The two *stupas* in Kathmandu, Phakpa Shingkun (Swayambunath), and Jharung Khashong (Bouddhanath), are considered by all Buddhists as very sacred shrines, and thousands come from all over Tibet, Nepal, and India to pay homage to these stupas. We met many of our old friends during the trip, and after a long tour, it was time for us to return. The weather was already beginning to get warm in India; we spent only a few days in Calcutta, then headed east.

It was in the beginning of March, 1958, when we arrived back in the small hill station of Kalimpong. The weather was beautiful; it is always very pleasant in the months of March and April. The air is fresh, there are few clouds, and one can see the snow mountains clearly. Mt. Kanchenjunga, standing magnificently across from where we were living, was our daily vista. Kalimpong used to be the main trade center between Tibet and India before the Chinese invasion of Tibet. Tibet's most successful export is wool, which was readily bought up by American companies, but after 1950, the United States Government banned the import of Tibet's wool because Tibet had come under Communist rule. Thus Kalimpong, as a trading town, became less important. Even so, the daily arrival of goods from Tibet and departure of goods to India continued until 1959. After 1959, a complete and total restriction of business and travel between India and Tibet was mutually pronounced by these countries.

That spring, notices to return home had been sent by the Tibetan Government to all officials who were staying in Kalimpong on the pretext of leave, and even others who had received no formal leave, like myself.

My father received notice too, advising him to return when his leave expired; however, he still had several months remaining. During his stay in Kalimpong, he worked a lot outside on the grounds, and we made a fairly good-sized vegetable garden. He tried to enjoy his stay, but could not help but worry about Tibet's situation and the children who had been left back in Lhasa. He mentioned often that the time had come for him to leave India and do some good work back home. The situation in Tibet was only worsening, and I tried to suggest to him that he should wait until conditions improved.

Meanwhile, Father and I paid visits to his friends in Darjeeling. Darjeeling is only twenty-nine miles from Kalimpong, but the road is narrow and very steep. One climbs about five thousand feet in an hour and a half to cover a distance of twelve miles. The roadside is blanketed with tea bushes where the famous teas of Darjeeling are grown. Magnificent views of the mountains can be seen from various altitudes while one climbs. Father remained about ten days in Darjeeling, meeting old friends. Among them were the Laden La family, whose father, the late W.D. Laden La, had been to Lhasa to assist Father in organizing the new police force. It was the best time of the year to visit Darjeeling, and we thoroughly enjoyed our stay.

A strange incident happened after we returned to Kalimpong. One day, a friend of ours known as Gyami Tsering, who was living in Kalimpong, invited us for lunch. The invitation was for our family, along with the Dorji family of Bhutan, but when we were about to take our seats at the table, the Chinese trade representative and his staff arrived. This was a very unwelcome surprise to all of us, for we had not been told that the Chinese trade representatives were to attend the party. Anyway, my father was a clever man; he never showed any sign of surprise upon seeing them. As for my wife and myself, we don't quite remember what we did. The awkward party then finished, and we were glad to be able to leave. The agreement on the frontiers of Tibet and India had been signed in 1952, and, as a result of this agreement, China had the privilege of establishing a trade mission at Kalimpong. The mission was closed after the 1959 revolt in Lhasa, completely cutting off trade between India and Tibet, and so there was no point in keeping the mission there for promoting trade. China's relations with India became increasingly strained following a border clash between Indian and Chinese troops on the northeast frontier and again in the Ladakh area in 1962.

It was time for Father's leave to expire, and he was anxious to return to Lhasa. One day he said to me that there was no point in staying in Kalimpong; instead, he could serve the Dalai Lama and his country better by returning to Lhasa, and there he could also look after the welfare of his children. He had made up his mind, and there was no way to stop him from going, so on September 19th, 1958, he left for Tibet. I suggested that I could leave my family in India and accompany him back, but this offer was flatly rejected. I did, however, accompany him as far as Gangtok. It was a sad parting, as I knew that it was quite possible I would never see him again.

My father visited His Holiness after his return, but I do not know what they discussed. Probably, he recommended that the Dalai Lama leave the country for the time being, as the Thirteenth Dalai Lama had done in 1910. He had told me about this intention before he left India. He prepared warm clothes, boots, and other equipment in case he had to make a sudden departure from Lhasa. I told him that he had now reached a certain age and should not consider himself to be as he was in 1910, when he put up such a strong resistance against the Chinese at Chaksam Ferry. When word got out that Father was departing Kalimpong for Lhasa, many friends and relatives came by to discourage him and plead that he delay his departure. But he would not listen to their suggestions. His reply was, "I have only a few years more to go; I am only flesh and bones. I am not afraid of dying. I must go because my leave is expiring. My foremost intention is to serve His Holiness and my country. I promised him that I would return, and it is my principle to keep my word." It was with these sentiments that he left.

During his return journey, Father halted a month or so in Dromo, staying in Rinchen Khang, a house belonging to family friends. My sister Mrs. Tess Dorji came to see him from Bhutan, trying to get him to return with her for a visit to Bhutan, but he refused the invitation, repeating his desire to return home. At this time, Pandit Nehru was to visit Lhasa in response to His Holiness the Dalai Lama's invitation, made during his visit to India in 1956. The Chinese said, however, that the situation in Tibet was such that it was not safe for the Prime Minister to visit Lhasa, and that they would not take responsibility for his personal safety. The visit did not work out, so instead, the Prime Minister went to Bhutan. He traveled via Dromo, Tibet; the direct road to the capital of Bhutan from the Indian side had not yet been constructed. As he was to pass through Tibet, the Tibetan Government sent a delegation led by Surkhang Shapé to Dromo. Surkhang Shapé was accompanied by a Chinese General, Tan Kun San, to welcome the Prime Minister of India. Tsarong, also being in Dromo at that time, was invited to the reception. My sister Mrs. Tsering Yangzom Taring, who was then residing in Lhasa, had come down to Dromo to meet Father and accompany him back. Together they were preparing to meet Pandit Nehru, but in his rush to reach the reception on time, Father slipped on a stairway and injured his hand, which began to bleed. He quickly wrapped it up, and they continued on their way. Once at the reception, my sister explained to the Prime Minister that her father was unable to shake his hands to welcome him. So Pandit Nehru walked up to Father and gave him a big embrace, which immensely pleased my father.

Father wrote me many letters from Dromo relating his experiences there. Once during a meeting he had with Surkhang Shapé and the Chinese General, the discussion became quite heated. The General pounded his fists on the table and shouted at Tsarong, "We will bring your son from Kalimpong back to Lhasa!" Father did not pay any attention to this threat and continued on his journey.

When Father decided to leave Dromo, his daughter Tess La packed a large box of food supplies to see them through the trip. My brother Phungen La rode in their truck, and my sister and Father went in the Land Rover. Together they started off towards

Phari, and although they arrived early, they did not remain but pushed on to Tuna. It was late at night when they arrived at the Dak Bungalow in Tuna; the truck was far behind. There were hardly any people around, and it was dark and quite cold. It was fortunate they had been sent with some supplies. In the morning they set off for Netod Estate, which lies between Gyantse and Shigatse; here they remained for two nights. Another sister from Gyantse came to visit Tsarong there, and he also met his old friend Doring, who was an officer in the military during the 1920s. The next stop was Shigatse, where Father halted for five nights at the house of Delek Rabten. The party then proceeded to Lhanga Estate. At Lhanga, the manager and all the servants had been notified of Father's visit, so when he arrived, they received him with a grand welcoming party. Everyone was in their best dress, and delicious foods had been prepared. As he approached the house, an attendant came with a traditional Tibetan offering called *dhroso-chemar*. This is a small tray, divided in two, one side piled high with wheat and the other with barley grain and butter. It is an auspicious offering for an important guest newly arriving; however, in this instance, as the attendant approached my father, the offering fell from his hands. Tibetans in general are somewhat superstitious, and this was clearly a bad omen for Father. His party stayed only one night at Lhanga and continued on to Lhasa.

Not far from the city, yet still on the Chang Thang, the group stopped for lunch in a small village called Markhyang. Many beggars and poor people approached them, and, as it was their last stop, my sister asked if she could give away the leftover food supplies. Father agreed, and she distributed the food. After all, they would be comfortably in their own home by that evening. With their truck already gone ahead, it was time for them to start the last leg of the journey. My brother Phungen La had stayed behind, so the three of them and the driver continued on in the Land Rover. Driving along the Chang Thang, the road became poor; the top layer was very sandy, and they soon experienced car trouble. At one point they were forced to stop and get out to push the car, and while doing this it somehow became overheated and caught fire. The driver also caught on fire, but he quickly got away and rolled in the sand; fortunately he escaped without injury. My sister and brother poured large amounts of sand into the car to extinguish the flames, which eventually died out, leaving the car completely inoperable. By this time it was dark, and they had no supplies, so they began walking to search for shelter. On the Chang Thang there are no houses; only with luck might one be able to find a tent belonging to the nomads who populated the plateau. The group began walking and Father suggested they all listen for dogs barking because where there were dogs, there were people close by. Being late October, it was cold and they had to walk for some time before they heard any dogs. Eventually, they came across a tent where they could take shelter for the night. Setting out early next morning, they were able to get a lift from a private truck making the last fifteen to twenty kilometers into Lhasa. They arrived home so early in the morning that everyone was fast asleep and no one was up to greet them. It was an extremely inauspicious way to arrive at one's home; in fact, there had been many poor signs during the return journey. Nevertheless, family members were happy to be reunited once again, and Father was pleased to have been able to keep his word to His Holiness.

8 Last Days

In late October 1958, at the time of my father's arrival in Lhasa, the atmosphere in the city was anxious and tense. People were afraid that anything might happen at any time. It was now known that many patriotic Tibetans were leaving for the south. This group included Tibetan troops as well as other individuals. The Chinese commanders were putting pressure on the Tibetan Government to send the Tibetan army to quell the rebels; but they themselves could not do so for fear that the troops would side with the rebels instead of putting them down. Constant meetings of the Cabinet Ministers and most unpleasant discussions with the Chinese took place; the city was thick with rumors and speculation.

Amidst all the difficulties, the Government was making great preparations for His Holiness's visit to Drepung, Sera, and Gaden Monasteries. It was time for him to take the final examinations for his Geshe degree, the highest degree one can receive in Tibetan religious study. Towards the end of 1958, His Holiness made his formal visits to these monasteries. According to the tradition, a grand procession of monks and lay officials, dressed in their best robes, escorted His Holiness out to Drepung Monastery. A great number of Tibetans lined the road, holding banners and burning incense, eager to receive his blessing. Each day of the ceremony, government officials were obligated to change their robes to different designs; this had been decreed by the Government in laws made long ago. Officials who later came to India told me that Tsarong had worn his very best brocade robes. They had teased him saying, "You put on a great show on this auspicious day." He replied, "Yes, this is a great day for all Tibetans, and this will be the last occasion for us to perform in this way."

❀ ❀ ❀

Indeed my father was a brave and battle-seasoned man. I remember during the power struggle between the two Regents seeing him go into a deep sleep while gunfire sounded throughout the city. Although he was known for having a hot temper, part of him always managed to keep calm and clear-headed during times of great distress; he had an ability to judge the situation for what it was. The evening he returned from Drikung District, when everyone panicked in fear of raids on their homes, he arrived from the two-day journey and immediately discussed the current situation with the family. He was certainly disturbed by it, and looked very tired. He went to bed earlier than usual, and my mother asked me to assist him. While I continued to relate to him the previous days' activity in Lhasa, he fell fast asleep despite the shooting that was still going on out in the streets!

Father seemed to be aware of the difficulties which lay ahead for both Lhasa and the country. He tried to arrange for his grandson Drikung Chetsang Rinpoche to be sent to India to join us. Rinpoche had come to Lhasa and was with my father when many people from the Drikung Monastery and District came to Tsarong House to voice their protest. As so many lamas had gone already, the Tibetans remaining behind were left without their spiritual advisors and teachers, a fearful thought considering the state of the country. The crowd outside had become quite hostile, exclaiming that Tsarong should not take their precious lama away from them, and that if he did, they would report him to the Government. With this, my father became very angry. He told them, "Very well, take Rinpoche back to Drikung immediately, but never regret this decision in the future."

Lhasa City was in a tense state when His Holiness the Dalai Lama's final examination for the Lharam Geshe Degree took place at the Tsuglak Khang. Over twenty thousand monks from the three great monasteries and all government officials attended the ceremony. When the Dalai Lama was coming from the Potala Palace to the Tsuglak Khang, two or three Chinese were arrested by the security men. They were carrying arms and were mingling with the crowds gathered to watch the procession; later those arrested were handed over to the Chinese authorities. This incident created much suspicion among the Tibetan people. His Holiness, having completed his examination successfully, was about to shift in a day or two from the Potala to the Norbu Lingka Summer Palace. Two junior Chinese officers arrived at the Tsuglak Khang inviting the Dalai Lama to watch a Chinese theatrical show at the army headquarters. They requested His Holiness to fix a time soon. The Dalai Lama could not fix a definite date given his busy schedule, but told them he would let them know after he returned to the Norbu Lingka. A day or so after His Holiness shifted, the Chinese authorities sent a reminder to the Norbu Lingka for him to fix a date to see the program. The Dalai Lama decided he would go on the 10th of March; it was 1959.

The invitation and the second request had taken place in such an urgent, hurried manner that it aroused suspicion on the Tibetan side. Similar incidents had occurred in eastern Tibet in which several high lamas and Khampa chiefs were invited to functions and had subsequently disappeared. These incidents were well known throughout the country, and people were very worried about this most recent, hasty move by the Chinese. Moreover, the day before the appointed date, the Chinese military headquarters called over the Bodyguard General, Kusang Depon, and warned him that no armed bodyguards would be allowed in the compound, only two or three unarmed guards. The Cabinet Ministers were also invited, but stern warnings were given that they should not bring more than one servant each and that they were not permitted to carry any arms with them. With these strict orders given to the Tibetan authorities, they were alarmed to the point of panic; the word was out among the people.

I later interviewed one Tibetan Government official, Tsewang Gyurmey Majha, who fled to freedom amidst the terrifying bombardment of the Potala and came to India through Kalimpong. He was a member of the Tibetan National Assembly and had witnessed the scene from beginning to end. He kindly gave me in writing the full account of the Lhasa revolt, which greatly helped me to understand the situation correctly.

By the evening of March 9th, everybody knew how serious things had become, and by the morning of the 10th, thousands of people began arriving at the palace gate to stop His Holiness from visiting the Chinese military headquarters. A potentially dangerous situation was developing. Tens of thousands were now gathered outside the walls of the Norbu Lingka Palace compound, shouting, "Tibet is our country," and "The Chinese must leave our country," thereby raising the tension almost to the point of a clash. By the order of the Dalai Lama, the ministers came out to speak to the crowd over a microphone telling them to calm down and leave at once for home. They told the crowd that representatives were leaving soon for the Chinese headquarters to inform the authorities there that His Holiness would not be coming and to appraise the current situation in order to prevent a serious riot. Some ministers then left and proceeded to the Chinese Military compound. They met with the Chinese officers led by General Tan Kun San, who was so enraged that he could hardly control his temper. He threatened to use his military might to crush the revolt once and for all. Yet the ministers were very polite and managed to calm him down with an assurance that they would try their very best to control the crowd. When the ministers returned to the Palace, they immediately reported to His Holiness, and everyone was distressed to hear what had taken place at the meeting with the Chinese.

The National Assembly was already in session, and several additional members joined in, having been elected by the people. The meeting was held at the Shapten Lhakhang (prayer hall) situated in the Norbu Lingka Palace compound where prayer meetings were usually conducted. Tsarong was present because he was the senior-most member of the National Assembly, but this time he was elected by the people, and the body of the Assembly now represented more a general public body than one appointed by the Government. The agenda of the meeting was, first, that the Assembly appoint a committee to organize a security force for the protection and safety of His Holiness the Dalai Lama. Second, it was essential that all people unite and strengthen their efforts to achieve the common objective. Thirdly, it was important to negotiate peacefully with the Chinese for our rights to our own land; and this must be told to the Chinese.

Members agreed that since this was an enlarged Assembly, the meeting place should be moved from the Palace to the Shol Enclave at the foot of the Potala Palace. Since there were so many people representing various parties, it was not possible to come to a meaningful conclusion; so they decided to form a smaller body, the number of which came finally to about sixty members.

While the National Assembly was in session at Shol, there were letters exchanged between His Holiness and General Tan Kun San. The General's first letter was polite and more diplomatic; but subsequent letters were just threats to crush the gathering of people at the Palace which included demands for a map showing where His Holiness was residing. It was becoming clear that the Chinese military was planning to use artillery to disperse the crowds, sparing His Holiness if they knew where he would be staying at the time. This, however, was a mere contrivance, and His Holiness's personal safety was placed at an extremely high risk.

The Chinese were bringing in troops by night to reinforce their established garrison there. They brought in tanks, artillery pieces, and armored vehicles in great numbers. Despite all the threats, people were determined to stay at the Palace, and no one, not even the Dalai Lama, could persuade them to return to their homes. This dangerous situation was reaching a climax and the Ministers and Secretaries approached His Holiness to advise him that the time had come for him to leave the Palace for a safer area, not only for his personal safety, but for the well-being of the country of Tibet as well. The Chinese fired two shells from the north side of the Norbu Lingka, which landed outside the Palace gate. This further influenced the Dalai Lama to leave immediately.

On the morning of March 17th, His Holiness consulted the Nechung oracle, who advised that he leave immediately, and promised that the Oracle would protect him. I believe that the Oracle did so, as there were thousands of Chinese troops posted around Lhasa; yet the direction in which the Dalai Lama chose to flee was free of all soldiers. The distance from the Palace to the crossing point at the southern riverside was about a mile, and it was first thought that they were taking a frightfully great risk, but somehow the whole party was able to cross the river without encountering any obstacles. It was astonishingly inconceivable that the Chinese would not have any troops patrolling in that direction. Even after crossing the river, the danger was not over, for there existed a large Chinese establishment at Norto Lingka, which was situated opposite the route taken by the Dalai Lama and his party. The distance between them was only a few hundred yards. The route winds along the mountainside beside the Kyichu River, curving inward to bring the party still closer to the Chinese camp. They could now see the lights at the encampment clearly, and many people were nervous because the clattering of horseshoes on the stony road and the noise of so many people moving by could easily alert the Chinese. There was a light wind blowing against the moving party; perhaps the noise was carried away along the river instead of being heard from the opposite bank. Whatever the reason, the Dalai Lama and his entourage managed to pass beyond the danger zone without any hindrance.

After the Dalai Lama's safe departure from Norbu Lingka, the National Assembly at Shol continued to shape a resolution to negotiate with the Chinese. Tsewang Gyurmey Majha, the Tibetan official who witnessed these meetings, gave me an account. He happened to meet my father several times when he was staying on the ground floor of a building that belonged to a monk official. Majha said that he remembered clearly what Tsarong had expressed as his opinion at this meeting. One thought was that it would be impossible to challenge the military power of the Chinese; instead, it would be better to organize guerrilla warfare and then seek assistance from foreign countries. He added, "If the Assembly agrees to this proposal, I shall be eager to do my best to work towards this aim. Our southern land is blessed with natural forest and we could easily fight the Chinese for a longer period, during which we shall have time to make our next move." Majha mentioned that what my father had proposed was a good idea, but unfortunately, a certain group strongly objected to it. Majha had felt that at this hour of crisis they needed a man like Tsarong, who had the vast experience of administration and command, and he was much disappointed by the decision not to take Tsarong's advice.

The Assembly then continued to draft a resolution to take to the Chinese authorities. Six members were elected to work on this resolution, and Tsarong was one of these six. Majha was also at this meeting and remembers some very useful points raised by Father. They agreed to approach the Chinese in two stages. However, before the talks could begin, the Chinese army started a heavy bombardment in the early morning of March 19th. Artillery shells were falling everywhere; there were no Chinese troops to be seen, and the Tibetans had to remain under cover. Talking to the Chinese authorities now seemed futile and everyone just remained hidden.

The last time Majha saw Tsarong, he was supervising volunteers in digging trenches. The situation soon became hopeless, and at dawn on the morning of March 22nd, Majha went up to the Potala through heavy fire, and was able to escape from the Palace. He did not witness the events thereafter.

The Chinese army started shelling the Norbu Lingka Palace at about two o'clock on the morning of the 19th, and continued for about five hours. Then, after a break of a few hours, shelling was resumed, and countless numbers of people were killed and injured in and around the Palace. In the afternoon, the survivors started moving out to escape to safety. People scattered to the north and south, the only possible routes of escape, only to be caught in heavy shelling and machine gun fire. Casualties were especially high by the riverside in the south, where many people were simply mowed down by machine guns. During the following three days of bombardment, thousands of Tibetans were killed in and around the city of Lhasa.

The Chinese entered the Norbu Lingka on the evening of the day the shelling began and arrested several senior officials of the Government who remained behind there in hiding. The Chinese were still shelling the Potala and the Chagpori Medical College when a barrage of shells fell in front of the Potala. A heavy cloud of red dust rose in front, totally covering the building. People who had witnessed this later told me that they thought that our treasured Potala was lost, but a little while later, as the building appeared through the dust, it seemed to have withstood the great shocks of the shells. This happened twice, and there was much damage done by the shells where they hit the building, though it appeared that nothing had affected the basic structure of the great Potala. The west wing, which housed the Namgyal Dratsang monks, was heavily damaged because Tibetan troops stationed there fired on the Chinese. At Shol, just below the Potala, it was a confusing and desperate scene, and everyone was of the mind to just surrender to the Chinese. They did so by raising white flags. At that moment of humiliation and despair, Father's thoughts must have flashed back to the early 1920s, when his army was strong and well-prepared with properly trained officers. He really must have been dismayed and disgusted.

The Chinese troops entered Shol and arrested all the leaders, including Tsarong. They were immediately taken to Norbu Lingka, and the next day all important leaders were marched to the Chinese army headquarters, where they were imprisoned. On their way, my father was exhausted and unable to walk further; he told the Chinese to shoot him on the spot, but they managed to get him to the army headquarters on horseback.

Days passed, and the prisoners were taken out in turn before the people of the city to face public humiliation. Many of them were beaten, scolded, and spat on by Tibetans. These Tibetans were recruited by the Chinese from among the bad characters bearing criminal records and dissatisfied people who had personal grudges against the individual prisoners. I learned later about two individuals who were selected by the Chinese to humiliate my father in his upcoming trial. One was a Muslim trader named Gulam Mohammed, and the other was my mother's maid, Dechen Chodon.

Gulam Mohammed was very well known to us, as he was one of our tenants. As previously mentioned, during the Second World War, the Tibetan Government permitted civil supplies for China to pass through Tibet. It was at that time that Gulam

Mohammed asked Tsarong to help him to send some velvet material to Kunming, China, with our own trade goods. Father willingly helped him by instructing his men to look after Gulam Mohammed's goods, consisting of about four mule loads. When our men returned to Lhasa, they brought with them Chinese silver dollars, arms and ammunition, and horses. It turned out to be very profitable, and Mohammed's goods did especially well. However, when the investment profits were distributed, he was given dollars, other trading goods, and animals in proportion. He would not accept this, wanting only dollars. He claimed it was an unfair deal and had even gone to court. Since that time he was strongly embittered against our family. After the Tibetan revolt was crushed in Lhasa, he left with many other Muslims, claiming that he was an Indian citizen from Kashmir. He passed through Kalimpong, and soon quietly left for Saudi Arabia, never returning to India.

The second person whom the Chinese chose to humiliate Father, Dechen Chodon, was from a poor family and my mother had helped her and kept her at our home. She was well looked after, and provided with clothes and ornaments. It was surprising to learn how she was willing to assist the Chinese. Later, our relatives who came out of Tibet told me that she was a demoniacal woman incited by the Chinese to turn against Father. During this time of great confusion, many people were humiliated by being made to parade around the city with long paper hats and strange costumes. It appeared somewhat comical, yet a dreadful fear was present at all times. Some prisoners were adorned with oracle, demon, or dancer's costumes, and were made to bow down before a crowd which was purposely selected from the worst elements of Lhasa society to abuse those on parade.

My father was kept in a prison cell with Dromo Geshe Rinpoche and Drungyik Chenmo Chophil Thubten, at that time the head of the ecclesiastical office under the Fourteenth Dalai Lama. Dromo Geshe Rinpoche was able to come to India later, and has a monastery in Kalimpong. During their captivity, three or four people were kept in each room and their legs were chained. Duties were delegated to the elderly people such as gardening or painting. Later, Father was moved to another room, together with Chophil Thubten. Father remained there for about three months, until the night before he was to be taken into the street for trial and public humiliation. His companion, Chophil Thubten, reported that Tsarong used to get up early every morning, but on the morning of his trial, he was very late in rising and when Chophil tried to wake him, was found to be dead. Father must have died quietly in his sleep, as no outcry or noise was heard by his cell mate or the prisoners in the neighboring quarters. His sudden death caused suspicion among the Chinese, and they took his body for autopsy. It was then handed over to his sister, Tsering Dolma, and her husband, Kusho Tsenam La. Tsenam La later sent a short note written on a piece of cloth and sewn to the lining of a woman's apron. In this way the message was brought to me by a Tibetan woman who escaped to India.

Our family never received any word of the autopsy results. Some people claim that, because of his timely death in the early morning before his scheduled trial, it appears he must have committed suicide. I strongly disagree with this assumption. Knowing well the nature of his character, I am sure he never would have done such a thing. It was told to me much later by a Tibetan refugee, who was with him on the evening before his death, that Tsarong appeared calm and friendly as usual. The prisoners had been allowed to mix that evening, as they were being shown a film. Tsarong sat watching the movie with his young grandniece on his lap and had offered one refugee his last cigarette.

❀   ❀   ❀

Many things have subsequently been written about my Father, but one thing that can never be disputed is that he was a loyal Tibetan until the end. He spent his entire life serving two Dalai Lamas and constantly strove to make Tibet a better country for all those who lived there, as well as making efforts to bring it forward into the international community. Some Tibetans believed he was Chagna Dorje, a Bodhisattva incarnate. It is evident that he had many qualities of one who works for the benefit of other beings. His death in a Chinese prison came as quite a shock to his family and friends, who both loved and respected him. Apart from this sad ending, I believe that the example of his life can be a great source of inspiration for all who pursue a free, productive, and peaceful life in their own homelands.